ARISE

Torn Curtain Publishing
Wellington, New Zealand
www.torncurtainpublishing.com

© Copyright 2023 Maree Cutler-Naroba. All rights reserved.

ISBN Softcover 978-0-6457827-1-4
ISBN Hardcover 978-0-6457827-2-1
ISBN EPub 978-0-6457827-3-8

No portion of this book may be reproduced, stored in a retrieval system or transmitted in any form or by any means—electronic, mechanical, photocopy, recording or otherwise—except for brief quotations in printed reviews or promotion, without prior written permission from the author.

Unless otherwise noted, all scripture is taken from the New International Version®, NIV®. Copyright © 1973, 1978, 1984, 2011 by Biblica, Inc.™ Used by permission of Zondervan. All rights reserved worldwide.

Scripture quotations marked NIrV are taken from the Holy Bible, New International Reader's Version®, NIrV® Copyright © 1995, 1996, 1998, 2014 by Biblica, Inc.™ Used by permission of Zondervan. All rights reserved worldwide. www.zondervan.com

Scripture quotations marked NLT are taken from the Holy Bible, New Living Translation, copyright © 1996, 2004, 2015 by Tyndale House Foundation. Used by permission of Tyndale House Publishers, Inc., Carol Stream, Illinois 60188. All rights reserved.

Scripture quotations marked NASB are taken from the New American Standard Bible®, Copyright © 1960, 1971, 1977, 1995, 2020 by The Lockman Foundation. Used by permission. All rights reserved. www.lockman.org

Scripture quotations marked NKJV are taken from the New King James Version. Copyright © 1982 by Thomas Nelson, Inc. Used by permission. All rights reserved.

Scripture quotations marked AMP are taken from the Amplified® Bible (AMPC), Copyright © 1954, 1958, 1962, 1964, 1965, 1987 by The Lockman Foundation. Used by permission. www.lockman.org

Typeset in Latino URW, Adobe Garamond Pro and Trajan Pro 3
Cover Image by Pixabay (Mark Robinson). Used with permission.

Cataloguing in Publishing Data
  Title: Arise: Awakening Christian Women Entrepreneurs to Shift the Course of History
  Author: Maree Cutler-Naroba
  Subjects: Women's Interests; Entrepreneurship; Christian Living; Spiritual Life;
      Spiritual Warfare; Business Strategies; Prayer; Leadership

A copy of this title is held at the National Library of Australia.

ARISE

Awakening Christian Women Entrepreneurs to Shift the Course of History

Maree Cutler-Naroba

ARISE

Awakening Christian Women Entrepreneurs to Shift the Course of History

Maree Cutler-Naroba

Contents

The Story of Deborah	1
Part One: Awake	7
Chapter 1 *She is Prayerful*	9
Chapter 2 *She is Prophetic*	21
Chapter 3 *She is Pioneering*	35
Chapter 4 *She is Visionary*	47
Chapter 5 *She is Mothering*	61
Part Two: Arise	73
Chapter 6 *She is Skilful*	75
Chapter 7 *She is Strategic*	85
Chapter 8 *She is Purposeful*	95
Chapter 9 *She is Encouraging*	107
Chapter 10 *She is Action-Oriented*	119
A Clarion Call to Modern-day Deborahs	131
Appendix: 5+U Pillars of Business Model	135
About the Author	145

The Story of Deborah

An Excerpt from the Book of Judges

(Chapters 4-5)

AGAIN THE ISRAELITES DID evil in the eyes of the Lord, now that Ehud was dead. So the Lord sold them into the hands of Jabin king of Canaan, who reigned in Hazor. Sisera, the commander of his army, was based in Harosheth Haggoyim. Because he had nine hundred chariots fitted with iron and had cruelly oppressed the Israelites for twenty years, they cried to the Lord for help. Now Deborah, a prophet, the wife of Lappidoth, was leading Israel at that time. She held court under the Palm of Deborah between Ramah and Bethel in the hill country of Ephraim, and the Israelites went up to her to have their disputes decided. She sent for Barak son of Abinoam from Kedesh in Naphtali and said to him, "The Lord, the God of Israel, commands you: 'Go, take with you ten thousand men of Naphtali and Zebulun and lead them up to Mount Tabor. I will lead Sisera, the commander of Jabin's army, with his chariots and his troops to the Kishon River and give him into your hands.'"

Barak said to her, "If you go with me, I will go; but if you don't go with me, I won't go." "Certainly I will go with you," said Deborah.

"But because of the course you are taking, the honour will not be yours, for the Lord will deliver Sisera into the hands of a woman." So Deborah went with Barak to Kedesh. There Barak summoned Zebulun and Naphtali, and ten thousand men went up under his command. Deborah also went up with him. Now Heber the Kenite had left the other Kenites, the descendants of Hobab, Moses' brother-in-law, and pitched his tent by the great tree in Zaanannim near Kedesh.

When they told Sisera that Barak son of Abinoam had gone up to Mount Tabor, Sisera summoned from Harosheth Haggoyim to the Kishon River all his men and his nine hundred chariots fitted with iron.

Then Deborah said to Barak, "Go! This is the day the Lord has given Sisera into your hands. Has not the Lord gone ahead of you?" So Barak went down Mount Tabor, with ten thousand men following him. At Barak's advance, the Lord routed Sisera and all his chariots and army by the sword, and Sisera got down from his chariot and fled on foot.

Barak pursued the chariots and army as far as Harosheth Haggoyim, and all Sisera's troops fell by the sword; not a man was left. Sisera, meanwhile, fled on foot to the tent of Jael, the wife of Heber the Kenite, because there was an alliance between Jabin king of Hazor and the family of Heber the Kenite.

Jael went out to meet Sisera and said to him, "Come, my lord, come right in. Don't be afraid." So he entered her tent, and she covered him with a blanket. "I'm thirsty," he said. "Please give me some water." She opened a skin of milk, gave him a drink, and covered him up. "Stand in the doorway of the tent," he told her. "If someone comes by and asks you, 'Is anyone in there?' say 'No.'" But Jael, Heber's wife, picked up a tent peg and a hammer and went quietly to him while he lay fast asleep, exhausted. She drove the peg through his temple into the ground, and he died.

Just then Barak came by in pursuit of Sisera, and Jael went out to meet him. "Come," she said, "I will show you the man you're looking for." So he went in with her, and there lay Sisera with the tent peg through his temple—dead.

On that day God subdued Jabin king of Canaan before the Israelites. And the hand of the Israelites pressed harder and harder against Jabin king of Canaan until they destroyed him.

∼

On that day Deborah and Barak son of Abinoam sang this song:

"When the princes in Israel take the lead, when the people willingly offer themselves—praise the Lord! Hear this, you kings! Listen, you rulers! I, even I, will sing to the Lord; I will praise the Lord, the God of Israel, in song.

When you, Lord, went out from Seir, when you marched from the land of Edom, the earth shook, the heavens poured, the clouds poured down water. The mountains quaked before the Lord, the One of Sinai, before the Lord, the God of Israel.

In the days of Shamgar son of Anath, in the days of Jael, the highways were abandoned; travellers took to winding paths. Villagers in Israel would not fight; they held back until I, Deborah, arose, until I arose, a mother in Israel. God chose new leaders when war came to the city gates, but not a shield or spear was seen among forty thousand in Israel.

My heart is with Israel's princes, with the willing volunteers among the people. Praise the Lord!

You who ride on white donkeys, sitting on your saddle blankets, and you who walk along the road, consider the voice of the singers at the watering places. They recite the victories of the Lord, the victories of his villagers in Israel.

Then the people of the Lord went down to the city gates. 'Wake up, wake up, Deborah! Wake up, wake up, break out in song! Arise, Barak! Take captive your captives, son of Abinoam.'

The remnant of the nobles came down; the people of the Lord came down to me against the mighty. Some came from Ephraim, whose roots were in Amalek; Benjamin was with the people who followed you. From Makir captains came down, from Zebulun those who bear a commander's staff. The princes of Issachar were with Deborah; yes, Issachar was with Barak, sent under his command into the valley. In the districts of Reuben there was much searching of heart. Why did you stay among the sheep pens to hear the whistling for the flocks? In the districts of Reuben there was much searching of heart. Gilead stayed beyond the Jordan. And Dan, why did he linger by the ships? Asher remained on the coast and stayed in his coves. The people of Zebulun risked their very lives; so did Naphtali on the terraced fields.

Kings came, they fought, the kings of Canaan fought. At Taanach, by the waters of Megiddo, they took no plunder of silver. From the heavens the stars fought, from their courses they fought against Sisera. The river Kishon swept them away, the age-old river, the river Kishon.

March on, my soul; be strong! Then thundered the horses' hooves—galloping, galloping go his mighty steeds. 'Curse Meroz,' said the angel of the Lord. 'Curse its people bitterly, because they did not come to help the Lord, to help the Lord against the mighty.'

Most blessed of women be Jael, the wife of Heber the Kenite, most blessed of tent-dwelling women. He asked for water, and she gave him milk; in a bowl fit for nobles she brought him curdled milk. Her hand reached for the tent peg, her right hand for the workman's hammer. She struck Sisera, she crushed his head, she shattered and pierced his temple. At her feet he sank, he fell; there he lay. At her feet he sank, he fell; where he sank, there he fell—dead.

Through the window peered Sisera's mother; behind the lattice she cried out, 'Why is his chariot so long in coming? Why is the clatter of his chariots delayed?' The wisest of her ladies answer her; indeed, she keeps saying to herself, 'Are they not finding and dividing the spoils: a woman or two for each man, colourful garments as plunder for Sisera, colourful garments embroidered, highly embroidered garments for my neck—all this as plunder?'

So may all your enemies perish, Lord! But may all who love you be like the sun when it rises in its strength."

Then the land had peace forty years.

Part One
AWAKE

CHAPTER ONE

She is Prayerful

'Mighty Deborah'. The word 'mighty' means: of extraordinary strength, power or influence. As a judge in ancient Israel, Deborah exemplified all of these. She was a woman who called on the Lord to be her strength, her guide, the source of wisdom and strategic understanding. Through her God, she accessed heavenly filing cabinets, obtaining blueprints and plans that showed the people of God what they were to do in the face of threat. In turn, Deborah spoke out those plans. Speaking to Barak, the commander of Israel's army at the time, she confidently conveyed the message: "Go, and take with you ten thousand men . . ."

Thankfully, Barak followed through on her words, and as a result, the course of history was shifted—all because of mighty Deborah, a woman of prayer who actioned what God told her. Prayer was like oxygen to Deborah; she did not want to do anything without God's guidance. In her weighty position as judge, she needed to lean on God for wisdom in every decision. Her dependency and reliance were on her heavenly Father.

Consider the people who came to Deborah to have her decide their case—it might have been someone who had stolen from a salesperson, or neighbours in conflict about their boundary lines. Not only that, the leaders of the land also consulted her regarding decisions that would affect the nation. Whatever the situation, Deborah needed to weigh each matter in her mind and heart, extending patience, tolerance, and understanding. In none of these cases could she afford to be flippant or make a judgement on a whim. In those moments, she needed to speak with the mind and heart of her heavenly Father.

As we read the book of Judges, we find Israel in a time of oppression. The nation had done evil in the sight of the Lord, and Ehud, the second judge of Israel, was dead. Still the nation continued to do evil in the sight of the Lord. In Judges 4 we read:

> *Again the Israelites did evil in the eyes of the Lord, now that Ehud was dead. So the Lord sold them into the hands of Jabin king of Canaan, who reigned in Hazor. Sisera, the commander of his army, was based in Harosheth Haggoyim. Because he had nine hundred chariots fitted with iron and had cruelly oppressed the Israelites for twenty years, they cried to the Lord for help.*
> — *Judges 4:1-3*

At this point in Israel's history, God's people had been slaves for twenty years. Worn down by the enemy's oppression, Israel, in a state of deep anguish and distress, finally cried out to the Lord to help them. In response, He raised up a woman called Deborah. Judges 4:4-5 tells us:

> *Now Deborah, **a prophet**, the wife of Lappidoth, was leading Israel at that time. **She held court** under the Palm of Deborah between Ramah and Bethel in the hill country of Ephraim, and the Israelites went up to her to have their disputes decided.*

The Lord saw His people choosing to turn to Him in the midst of their pain and suffering, and sent help—this time, through an incredible woman of God—Deborah, a woman of courage who walked in obedience to the Father, a woman mighty in faith. Deborah was a leader who communed deeply with God as she sat in judgement over Israel; she relied on His guidance to navigate the many complex decisions placed in her hands. Prayer was her lifeline.

As we begin exploring the life of Deborah, the first thing we discover is that her prayers were a catalyst to history being changed and the plans and purposes of God being fulfilled. Her prayers brought heaven to earth, freedom and peace in place of chaos and conflict. In prayer, Deborah tuned her ear to hear what her Father was saying, and positioned her heart to move in obedience, confidence, and wisdom. From His presence, she was able to action all that God had spoken to her.

∽

A modern-day Deborah is one whose life is characterised by prayer; she is given to praying. When we surrender to God, seeking that His will be done, we are drawn into His presence in worship, prayer, and praise. As we go about our daily lives, it is easy to forget that our actions—our work, our business, our parenting and so on—need to flow out of the time we spend with our Father. God calls us to partner with Him to see His kingdom come here on earth, and He longs for us to commune with Him in prayer—just as Deborah did.

I have seen the power of prayer. As I was approaching the end of my studies at Teachers College, I was seeking the Lord about where I was to go for my first teaching post. I was studying in Christchurch at the time, and I wanted to go back to Wellington, where I had been previously, completing my commerce degree. As a new Christian in Wellington, I had flourished in my walk with God and was part of an amazing church family. I particularly loved the bible classes I attended most weeks. Those early years of learning what it meant to be in a relationship with God rather than pursuing religion, and discovering that His Word was a lamp for my feet and a light to my path (Psalm 119:105), were foundational to my journey with God.

While I waited on the Lord about where to take a job, I began applying for various teaching posts around the country, asking Him to show me which one to accept (all the while thinking *could it please be Wellington?!*). I clearly remember one morning in late November when the phone in my flat rang. It was the principal from Cambridge High School, wanting to ask me a few questions. A few minutes later, he offered me a job on the spot. I asked if I could call back within the next few days, but as I walked back to my bedroom, all I could think was, *but it's not Wellington.*

As I prayed, God spoke to me from John 10:27: "My sheep hear my voice, and I know them, and they follow me." At that moment I knew without a doubt the Lord was stamping a 'yes' on taking this teaching role. I did not know one person in Cambridge; in fact, I had to look up where it was. As it turns out, Cambridge was seven hours' drive from Wellington. But God had spoken, and as I confidently stepped into the role the following year, God miraculously provided accommodation, a church home, friendships and more—all through connections I had made during my time in Wellington!

~

It was almost twenty years later that God started whispering to my heart about the story of Deborah. I had read the book of Judges at various times, and always loved that Deborah was a bold and courageous woman. This time, however, the Lord led me to do a more in-depth study of Judges 4 and 5. As I did so, I found myself jotting down ideas and thoughts about creating a Deborah-themed conference for Christian women entrepreneurs. In prayer, God began speaking to me about taking the conference to the nation—and then to the nations. He also gave me fresh revelation about the life of Deborah. He showed me how the lessons we learn from her life, and her characteristics, could relate to women in business. I knew that God was calling businesswomen to rise as modern-day Deborahs who participate in shifting the course of history.

Within a year, the first *Deborah Conference* was launched. Since then, it has become an annual event. Each year we have a specific theme, with workshops and keynote sessions led by speakers who inspire and equip Christian women entrepreneurs to pursue their business with passion and purpose, wrapped in God's presence.

The launch of the *Deborah Conference* was a faith-action birthed in prayer. Back then, I did not have everything all in a straight line or all the details worked out. There were a lot of unknowns, and yes, I did feel hesitant and anxious at times. But it was in the 'prayer closet' that God gave me peace and reassured me that He was in control and would show me the way in which I should go (Psalm 32:8).

Today, the Deborah Conference has been held in-person in all major centres of Australia and online, reaching into rural communities and around the world. It's a challenge to see ourselves as *Mighty Deborahs* who understand the global impact we can have as Christian women in business.

How many situations can you think of right now—in your family, your business, your country, or around the world—that are burdened by conflict and chaos? Will you give yourself to a life of prayer that pulls on the resources of heaven, summons the angels to their assignments, and unlocks the keys, plans and strategies that allow freedom and peace to reign?

Prayer is a conversation between us and our heavenly Father. God is not counting how many minutes we pray for, or listening to see whether our sentence structure is right. In fact, prayer can take many forms. At times, my prayers have simply been buckets and buckets of tears. I love Psalm 56:8, where we read, "You keep track of all my sorrows. You have collected all my tears in your bottle. You have recorded each one in your book" (NLT).

Cultivating a Prayerful Spirit

Prayer is simply talking with our heavenly Father. Yet many people find prayer a struggle. If that is you, I suggest using the Lord's Prayer as a starting point. It's found in Matthew 6, and begins with these words: "This, then, is how you should pray . . ." (v. 9). Let's look at some ways we can cultivate a prayerful spirit like Deborah.

Come with Praise

"Our Father in heaven, hallowed be your name, your kingdom come, your will be done on earth as it is in heaven.'" (v. 10)

Isn't it striking that the very first lines of the Lord's Prayer call us to praise? "Hallowed be Your name"—in other words, *We praise You, God! From the rising of the sun to the going down of the same, Your name is to be praised! (Psalm 113:3). We worship You in spirit and in truth! (John 4:23-24).*

Begin your time of prayer with praise, worshipping with thankfulness for all our God has done. Thank Him that all things are in His hands and that because of what Jesus has done we can enter through the veil and come boldly before His throne of grace. We can come right into His presence, where there is fullness of joy and pleasures for evermore (Psalm 16:11). Our Father in heaven delights in us coming to Him to prayer. He is waiting for us. He does not cast out those who come to Him (John 6:37). But let's be sure to first and foremost come before Him with praise.

Come Daily

Give us today our daily bread. (v. 11)

To me, one of the key words in the Lord's Prayer is the word 'daily'. Today's worries are sufficient for today—in fact, His Word teaches us not to be anxious about our tomorrows, for tomorrow will worry about itself (Matthew 6:34). As business owners, there is always more to be done. I don't know about you, but I find my action list is never empty. I cross off some things, but others then get added on. As I pray, this scripture reminds me that He will be present with me *today*, that I can ask for what I need *today*, and that my worries, burdens and thoughts about my 'tomorrows' can be placed at His feet. Over and over I am reminded that His mercies are new every morning, and great is His faithfulness (Lamentations 2:23-24). So go ahead! Thank Him *for today;* ask Him for provision *for today.*

Come for Forgiveness

And forgive us our debts, as we also have forgiven our debtors. (v. 12)

This part of the Lord's prayer shows us the need to ask the Lord's forgiveness for our words, our ways, and any acts that have not been pleasing to Him. Psalm 19:14 calls us to pray that the words of our mouths and meditations of our hearts be acceptable in His sight. We are also to forgive those we hold any angst, anger or irritation towards. In forgiving others, we release them back to the Father, the One who is able to work in people's hearts in ways we may never fully understand. We are called to lay down those who have grieved us or hurt us badly, along with circumstances and situations that have been incredibly unfair, before our loving Father, even through our tears. Romans 12:19 reminds us that vengeance belongs to the Lord. It is God who will sort out even the most complex and painful of situations for us. We are simply called to do our part by receiving—and extending—forgiveness.

Come Ready for Battle

And lead us not into temptation, but deliver us from the evil one. (v.13)

In this hour, we are to stay focussed on our God. There *is* evil in the world. We *do* have an enemy. We must be aware, however, that our battle is not against flesh and blood, but against principalities and powers. In prayer we are to put on the battle armour He has given us: the breastplate of righteousness, the shield of faith, the two-edged sword of His Word, the helmet of salvation, the belt of truth, and shoes which carry the good news (Ephesians 6:10-18).

Let's be women who go into each day's battle clothed in armour, but also knowingly clothed in glory! We read, "Now if we are children, then we are heirs—heirs of God and co-heirs with Christ, if indeed we share in his sufferings in order that we may also share in his glory" (Romans 8:17).

We will prevail, and God will give us strength for whatever we face during the day. We will not be like those of Ephraim who turned away in the heat of the battle (Psalm 78:9). Instead, like Deborah, we can go into battle knowing God is the victor, and in Him, we have the victory. We are surrounded with songs of deliverance! (Psalm 32:7). For this reason we can joyfully finish our time in prayer with the words, "Yours is the kingdom and the power and the glory, forever and ever, Amen!" (v. 14).

IN THAT MOMENT

Glory, glory, I sense the glory!
His love is so intense
I am brought to my knees,
Yet so refreshing.

As He reaches out to me,
I bow my head in awe.

Who am I but a battle-weary soldier
kneeling before my King?
But in this moment all my
fears and anxieties are swept away.
His eyes of warmth and of fire still me.
He whispers: "Warrior, do not doubt."

His glory rises, swirls, and dances upon me.
My soul knows: *I can be strong in the One I have found*
Indeed, I am standing on holy ground.

While it is true that we are always taking ground in prayer, we must be mindful not to fall into the habit of thinking we need to be 'on the battlefield' constantly. Every soldier needs to rest and refresh. That is why we read, "Those that wait upon the Lord shall renew their strength, mounting up with wings as eagles, they shall run and not be weary; they shall walk and not faint" (Isaiah 40:31).

As we reflect on the life of Deborah, I want us to cultivate a practise of 'pause and ponder'. Take moments to do just that, to pause and ponder—to *selah*—as you consider what it would have been like for the Israelites at that time in their history. As you read the book of Judges, ask yourself, *What would Deborah have been feeling and experiencing? What was God doing during this period?*

Judges is quite a challenging book to read as it is filled with war and fighting. It can feel quite exhausting as you work your way through it, and in some ways, you probably want to rush to get it over and done with! But Hebrews 4:12 tells us that the Word of God is powerful, and Isaiah 55:11 says that the Word of God does not return void. God wants us to chew slowly on His Word. It is not like there are parts of the bible that are simply there for the sake of adding words. No, each scripture is there to bring us into a revelation of who the Father is, and who the Father has called us to be. So practise the pause and ponder—*selah*—moments!

Deborah was a woman who was confident in her God. That confidence came from a deep and abiding relationship with her heavenly Father, forged through a life of prayer. When the crisis came, Deborah was there ready to be used by the Lord. To be in that place of readiness, as Deborah was, implies that she knew how to hear His voice and to recognise what He was leading and guiding her to do.

Deborah was clearly used to leaning in close to the whispers of the Father. Take a pause and ponder moment with a verse from Judges 5:

> *"May all your enemies perish, Lord! But **may all who love you be like the sun when it rises in its strength**." Then the land had peace forty years. (v. 31)*

"May all who love you be like the sun." Think about the sun—it is powerful; it brings the day, a new dawn. It is consistent; as the sun rises, so it sets, and then rises again the next day. Our prayer lives need to be like the sun—day in and day out, consistent and persistent.

Strengthening your prayer walk comes through spending time consistently and persistently in prayer. Remember the story of the man who kept knocking on his friend's door until his friend (representing Jesus) answered? He did this because he had no 'bread'—no revelation, no insight, no answers—but his friend did! (Luke 11:5-13). Through being prayerful, you will have peace in your heart, and you will be prepared and ready to step into the adventures God has for you.

Reflection Questions

1. How is your prayer life currently?

2. Write out a scripture that encourages you to be persistent in your prayer life.

3. What two steps will you take to strengthen your prayer walk in the next thirty days? There are some excellent apps that can help you with this. I like using the *Prayer Mate* app to create lists of prayer areas/topics.

4. As a woman in business, what are two ways in which you could incorporate consistent prayer into your day? For example, I have a prayer chair in the corner of my office that I go and sit on to cultivate intentional *selah* moments during my day.

CHAPTER TWO

SHE IS PROPHETIC

IN THE BEAUTIFUL KIMBERLEY area of Northwest Australia where I currently reside, the sun begins to rise between 4.30 a.m. and 5 a.m. each day. There's no need to set an alarm for an early start, however, because the sunrise is always preceded by the most incredible birdsong. Every morning the birds wake just before dawn and pour out their song. It's as if they want to tell the world that they have risen, and remind everyone that they are every bit as powerful in the new day as they were when they went to bed. Their loud warbling is also a signal of their strength and dominion—they don't want other birds moving into their territory!

Birdsong represents confidence, optimism, and hope for the future. As such, the birdsong serves as a prophetic call, much like the words of Jeremiah 29:11:

> *"For I know the plans I have for you," declares the Lord, "plans to prosper you and not to harm you, plans to give you hope and a future."*

Birdsong is a wonderful metaphor for the prophetic because it shows the purpose of our faith-filled declarations. We are not meant to be silent. Instead, like the birds, our lives are to be lived out loud to the glory of God!

Listen to Deborah's 'birdsong':

> On that day Deborah and Barak son of Abinoam sang this song: "When the princes in Israel take the lead when the people willingly offer themselves—praise the Lord! Hear this, you kings! Listen, you rulers! I, even I, will sing to the Lord; I will praise the Lord, the God of Israel, in song.
>
> The voice of the singers at the watering places. They recite the victories of the Lord, the victories of his villagers in Israel. Then the people of the Lord went down to the city gates. 'Wake up, wake up, Deborah! Wake up, wake up, break out in song! Arise, Barak! Take captive your captives, son of Abinoam."
>
> — *Judges 5:1-3, 11-12*

In these scriptures we witness Deborah praising God and glorying in what He had done—even before the victory was won! It is a clear example of her confidence in the Lord. Deborah knew that whenever God's people went into battle, God went out ahead of them.

Many years before, God had commanded the children of Israel to remove the carved images and idols out of Canaan and demolish all the high places there. He commanded them to take possession of the land of Canaan and settle in it, because He had given it to them to occupy (Numbers 33:52-53).

However, when the children of Israel crossed over the Red Sea, they didn't simply walk into the new land and settle down; they had to go to battle and occupy it. For this, they were given a birdsong, a battle cry of victory in the Lord. They were to make their voices heard as they took possession of the land.

Like the Israelites, God has commissioned us to take territory for Him and to safeguard it. But like Deborah, we must rise each day to hear the voice of the Lord and proclaim His greatness as He speaks to us of the spiritual 'land' we are to possess. I love the words of Isaiah 50:4: "The Sovereign Lord has given me a well-instructed tongue, to know the word that sustains the weary. He wakens me morning by morning, wakens my ear to listen like one being instructed."
Listen to the instruction Deborah received and passed on to Barak:

Then Deborah said to Barak, "Go! This is the day the Lord has given Sisera into your hands. Has not the Lord gone ahead of you?" So Barak went down Mount Tabor, with ten thousand men following him.
— *Judges 4:14*

Deborah knew how to operate prophetically. In God, Deborah had a perspective on Israel's circumstances. She knew that "to everything there is a season, and a time for every matter or purpose under heaven" (Ecclesiastes 3:1). Her prophetic words carried authority. Why? It was because of her relationship with God. Deborah's words had heavenly, life-changing power because through prayer, her own life was plugged in to the greatest power source this world will ever know! Her life rested in knowing who she was, who she was called to be, and whose authority she sat under—that of her God. Because of this, Deborah was able to fully express herself, her love for God, her confidence in Him, and her vision of the future.

At the time, however, the future looked uncertain. Israel was in a season of great trouble when Deborah came into position as a judge and a prophet. But God placed a burden on her heart for the people. As she drew near to God, she experienced God's desire for His people. Seeing them in distress, her heart's cry was doubtless,

"Surely, Lord, something must be done."

The Lord responded to Deborah as she sought Him about the time and season she found herself in. God told her to speak a strong word to Barak, which I take the liberty of paraphrasing as: "Barak, get yourself and the army moving right now—go!"

Barak's response was completely unexpected. "If you go with me," he replied, "I will go; but if you don't go with me, I won't go!"

Listen to mighty Deborah's courageous, confident reply:

> *"Certainly I will go with you," said Deborah. "But because of the course you are taking, the honour will not be yours, for the Lord will deliver Sisera into the hands of a woman."*

Sure enough, Deborah accompanied Barak into battle—along with the ten thousand men he summoned and placed under his command (Judges 4:8-10).

As we study the life of Deborah, it is helpful to differentiate between the *office* (or role) of prophet and the *gift* of prophecy. Someone in the 'office' of a prophet, like Deborah, has a mandate to speak forth what will happen in the future and to give strategic direction. In scripture we see many examples of the office of prophet, such as Moses and Jeremiah. In Deuteronomy 18:18 God tells Moses, "I will raise up for them a prophet like you from among their fellow Israelites, and I will put my words in his mouth. He will tell them everything I command him." To Jeremiah, the Lord said, "I have put my words in your mouth" (Jeremiah 1:9).

Not all of us carry a prophetic mantle like this, but in 1 Corinthians 14, Paul urges everyone to pursue the *gift of prophecy*. The purpose of the gift of prophecy is to encourage, exhort, and lift others up. In 1 Corinthians 14:3 we read: "But the one who prophesies speaks to people for their strengthening, encouraging and comfort." We see this gift operating in Deborah—she didn't merely speak God's direction to Barak in her role as prophet and then pull back. No, she went on to encourage Barak that he indeed could do that which God was calling him to. Deborah could see in Barak what he could not see in himself, and with the gift of prophecy she strengthened and encouraged him. In my eyes, this is the central pillar of the prophetic: to exhort and encourage, to call out the potential, the dreams, the 'gold' that God has placed in each person.

As modern-day Deborahs, we too are to operate prophetically. We are called to edify and lift others up through the words we speak and write, and the actions we take. Some modern-day Deborahs may also move in the office of prophet, but not all. God gifts us in different ways. And yet we can all take heed of Paul's encouragement to pursue the gift of prophecy. As we work in our given roles or manage our business ventures, let's be on the lookout for ways to strengthen and champion those we interact with each day, tuning our heart to the promptings and prophetic insights God has for us.

Let me share with you a time when God spoke prophetically to me. I had recently moved from New Zealand to Australia when I felt God put on my heart to start a meet-up group for businesswomen in my new city. Even though I knew it would be a great way to grow my friendships and network, I thought, *Goodness God, I don't know anyone here in Adelaide!* All the same, I stepped out in faith, produced some promotional material, wrote some social media posts, booked a venue, and waited with expectation . . .

The first night of our meet-up, I was amazed. God brought along a group of complete strangers who, within minutes, became great friends and business colleagues. Many years later, I am still in contact with some of these women and am still in awe of what God did as I responded to the prophetic prompting in my heart. In fact, I would often drive home after a meet-up feeling like I was almost floating, thinking *how did that happen?!*

But it wasn't just the group God was had in mind—it was each individual who came. One particularly cold winter evening, only a handful of us had come along. We started a pairs-sharing activity, when out of the corner of my eye I noticed a woman enter the room. Her head was slightly down, her steps hesitant. She was enveloped in a coat and clutched a handbag tightly to her body. I went over to her and gave her a big hug as I greeted her. It just seemed that was the thing to do in that moment; in response, her head lifted somewhat, and I saw a small smile emerge. I found her a seat at the table and introduced her to a couple of the other women. The next day I received a text from her—I still remember it to this day.

> *Maree, I'm an introvert, and I know as a business owner I need to get out more. Last night I forced myself to come. I sat in my car and told myself I would try for just five minutes, and if I couldn't handle it I would walk out. I was so nervous. You met me within a second of me coming in the door and your hug melted my heart—I could feel your care and love. You gathered me into the group, welcoming me with your words, and that was it, I was all in! See you next month! I am so encouraged.*

This is the power of operating in the prophetic! When we are clear about what God is saying, like Deborah, we can step out bravely and boldly, and as we implement what He tells us, others will be encouraged. Let's be women who say, "Lord, what is on your heart for this place, for these people, for this situation? Lord, what is the direction, the changes that need to take place? What is it that you want me to say and do about the things or people you have put on my heart?" Like Deborah, let's lean into the heart of the Father, resting in His presence, hearing His whispers, then going forth to edify, exhort and encourage others with our words and actions, knowing that God will move!

In turn, God will encourage and strengthen us. As we tune into God and release His words, we will find them 'hitting the mark' in astounding ways! In my coaching and consulting practice I have had numerous occasions when a client has reflected, "Wow, how did you know that about me?" or "I was amazed at how you wove all that I talked about into the business plan you wrote. You can see exactly what I want to do in my business and sorted my jumbled mess into a plan." How does this happen? It's because God moves in and through us in our everyday lives, whether we are functioning in our role as mums, aunties, bankers, songwriters, business owners or whatever it may be.

I tell you this because I want you to know that being prophetic goes beyond what is spoken from a platform or through a microphone in the setting of a church service. While this is one way prophecy can be delivered, the prophetic is also for the marketplace. So ask God daily to show you what is on His heart for a person, place or situation, and what would He have you to speak, write, or do to release it.

It is never a waste to share prophetic words that God has for people's lives. I have often spoken a word, only to find that years later that person has come back to me and said, "Remember when you said X and Y? Well, it has happened—I am now doing X and Y!" To be honest I don't always remember what I prophetically spoke, and I don't necessarily need to, as God will always have His way. But those times have encouraged me to keep seeking the Father's heart, His wisdom, and His compassion, so that when opportunities arise,

I may speak with accuracy, bringing direction, encouragement and comfort to the listeners.

Cultivating a Prophetic Spirit

Deborah was centred in her prayerful relationship with the Father and knew how to speak prophetically into specific times and seasons. We too must lean into God, seeking the right moment to speak, write or act on that which He has given us, be it for a nation or a specific person, or regarding a business idea. There are also some practical ways we can grow, both in the office of a prophet and in the gift of prophecy.

Soak Constantly in the Word of God

The prophetic must be rooted and anchored in the Word of God. Be hungry for the Word of God. Grow in your depth and understanding of scripture across the Old and New Testaments—don't just cherry pick! Read the hard parts; seek God's heart as to what was He doing at that time in history, what was He revealing to His people. In Job 23:12 we read: "I have not departed from the commands of his lips; I have treasured the words of his mouth more than my daily bread." In Psalm 1:2 we are told that the blessed man finds his delight "in the law of the Lord, and on his law he meditates day and night."

As you study the biblical prophets, notice the way in which God spoke to them and the way in which they implemented or activated what God said. What were the characteristics of their life in God? What was their character like? What areas did God need to correct them on?

Read Books and Listen to Podcasts on the Prophetic

There are many great books and podcasts available to help you develop your understanding of the prophetic—what it means, what it doesn't mean, where prophets have erred, where prophets have brought breakthrough because they spoke out what God had told them. There is teaching available on how God uses prophets in different ways, how the prophetic gift does not require you to say 'thus saith the Lord' on the end of every sentence you prophesy. There is much to glean and to learn!

Intentionally Expand Your Heart

To know the seasons and times of God we need to have a macro view, looking upwards and outwards, being intentional about seeking the bigger picture. As prophets, we can't afford to bury our heads in the sand or only be looking downwards, inwards, or with a micro view of situations, places, people and nations. We must constantly ask, *what is going on from God's perspective?*

I have a large world map on the wall in my office. Each day I look at that map and I declare, "God, show me what is it that you are doing among the nations. Lord, I hear of wars and floods and famines. What have you to reveal for this nation, or that people-group?" God is coming back for *every* nation—all tribes, peoples and languages; not one will be forgotten. Our prophetic hearts are stirred as we read Revelation 7:9, "After this I looked, and behold, a great multitude that no one could number, from every nation, from all tribes and peoples and languages, standing before the throne and before the Lamb, clothed in white robes, with palm branches in their hands."

I believe that if we first seek God's heart for nations—the bigger picture—God will be faithful to reveal the smaller picture as well—

the cities, towns, communities, people, places and situations we are to release His words over. He will reveal what we are to speak, what we are to write, what we are to do. Out of the macro will flow the micro.

Practise Prophecy

Make it a daily practise to exhort, encourage and lift others up. Remember, this is the purpose of the prophetic. So, notice what God is putting on your heart for a particular person—then send a message or note of encouragement or comfort to them. Think of practical ways you can nurture and champion others. How can you sow into their God-given dreams and hopes? When you edify and exhort others, it activates what God has put in them; it validates the talents and skills that God has gifted them with. Never underestimate the power of encouraging people, even in small ways. A smile and a warm greeting goes a long way in a world where more and more people are challenged with anxiety, depression, loneliness and disconnection.

Link Arms with Other Prophetic People

In the Bible, prophets often worked together. In 1 Samuel 10:10 we read that when Saul and his servant arrived at Gibeah, "a procession of prophets met him; the Spirit of God came powerfully upon him, and he joined in their prophesying." This procession could also be referred to as a 'company of prophets'. Being around others who are like-minded and similarly gifted will help sharpen and hone your own gifts. Proverbs 27:17 tells us, "As iron sharpens irons, so one person sharpens another."

Link 'arms' with other prophetic men and women and learn from them. Glean from the way they move in the prophetic; notice where God uses them prophetically. As a new believer seeking to expand my understanding of the prophetic and its purpose, I remember a visiting minister came to our church and he taught on the topic of prophecy. As I listened, I felt a desire, a pull, a nudging from the Holy Spirit, that God wanted me to grow in this particular area of my life and I needed to be intentional in doing so. I was to learn and glean from those God was already using in the prophetic space.

There are many incredible women around the world who God has anointed in the office of a prophet. I read, listen, and gain wisdom from their ministry. Equally I am privileged to know many women who move strongly in the gift of prophecy who are bankers, teachers, mothers and businesswomen simply going about their everyday lives. From the moment you get around these women they exhort, encourage, and edify. I love hanging with them when I can. There have been times when I have felt a leap in my spirit as it were, like Elizabeth when Mary met her (Luke 1:41), when I meet such women. It is exciting to find others who share the same desire to grow in this area of our lives.

Tune in to What Moves Your Heart the Most

One of the ways we begin to function prophetically is to tune in to the things that move us in our spirit. Notice the situations that move you to tears, or to anger, or to action. Think of it as a 'holy provocation'—big emotions or unexpected responses are often a signal that God's Spirit is also moved to action. Perhaps you feel compelled to give money to the homeless people you see on the footpath, or to smile at young children who look sad. God has given all of us knowledge, compassion and passion for certain people and situations.

One area that moves my heart hugely is seeing children distressed and neglected. I pick up on those situations quickly, see the red flags, sense and feel easily what is going on in ways other people might not see. When I am moved in this way I ask God for wisdom and insight. I ask questions like, "Lord, is there something I need to do right now? Is there something I can say that will help this person or situation?"

When we operate in the prophetic and are aware of how His Spirit moves us, we find ourselves stepping into situations at just the right time and place. So, notice what moves your heart—and respond with confidence. We will not all be moved by the same thing; God uses us all in different ways. Seek His heart to know what He is moving your heart for the most.

Don't Hold Back

It takes courage to step out prophetically. Think of Deborah. As the first and only female judge of Israel, releasing the word of the Lord to a male in authority was not an easy thing to do. That certainly would have required bravery, and a confidence that her message was straight from God Himself. And yet she did not hold back. She knew the prophetic word needed to be released.

As modern-day Deborahs, I believe we are all called to write or speak out in some shape or form. Some of us will write books, poems, and songs; others will speak at conferences and various events. For you it might be the words spoken to clients and customers, or the vision or the social media posts you are to write for your community. Remember, the heart of God has many facets and many expressions. For some, the prophetic 'words' God will release through you will be in the form of painting, sculpting, dancing, or another other art form.

Each of us has Kingdom influence through the power of our words. Some of my favourite words are those of the prophet Jeremiah:

> *But if I say, "I will not mention his word or speak any more in his name," his word is in my heart like a fire, a fire shut up in my bones. I am weary of holding it in; indeed, I cannot.*
> — *Jeremiah 20:9*

It is my prayer that God's Word would so burn in us that we grow weary of containing it, to the point where the only thing we can do is courageously release the words God has given us! Certainly there are times we need to tuck away what He has given us, allowing Him to gradually unfold what He is revealing to us. But we should never make this an excuse for holding back. When God tells us to do something, simply go and do it! When He gives a word, speak it out!

I believe we are living in an hour of the birdsong. It is time for the modern-day Deborahs to awake! So rise up, mighty Deborahs, and sing your song! Sing out what is in the heart of God, knowing that your 'birdsong' is one of victory.

Reflection Questions

1. Is there a particular nation, industry or demographic that God has placed on your heart? What moves your heart the most?

2. What could you do to familiarise yourself with the nation, industry, or demographic He has placed on your heart?

3. Sit with God awhile. Ask Him to give you a scripture or scriptures for the people or places He has highlighted to you. Write out the scriptures and begin praying them over the people, places or situations God has laid on your heart.

4. Ask God for wisdom and open doors to speak in whatever ways He would have you express what He has shown you.

CHAPTER THREE

She is Pioneering

When we hear the word 'pioneering', our mind often jumps to the likes of Sir Edmund Hillary, the first man to climb Mount Everest, the amazing Mother Teresa who gave her life to serve those in deep poverty, Alexander Graham Bell, who invented the first telephone, or Henry Ford who produced the first car . . . I'm sure you have your own mental list of such people. 'Pioneering' is a word that can intimidate us, given the calibre of people it brings to mind. They are usually those who are the first to use a new method, or apply an area of knowledge, or engage in a particular activity. They are the progressives, the ones we think of as 'ahead of their time'.

My favourite synonym for pioneering is 'trailblazing'. There is no doubt Deborah was a trailblazer. Strengthened by her God, Deborah rose with courage and fortitude and took hold of the gifts in her hands, the mantle upon her life, and the opportunities that the Lord put before her to take territory for Him. This was necessary at this point in Israel's history, because they had begun *losing* territory. But Deborah issued a 'trailblazing' command and encouragement to take back what had been lost to them. We read that she sent for Barak and said to him:

> *"The Lord, the God of Israel, commands you: 'Go, take with you ten thousand men of Naphtali and Zebulun and lead them up to Mount Tabor. I will lead Sisera, the commander of Jabin's army, with his chariots and his troops to the Kishon River and give him into your hands.'"*
>
> — *Judges 4:6-7*

Barak and his army went up to take possession of the land, and as a result, Israel's enemy was not only subdued but ultimately destroyed. Thanks to Deborah's pioneering spirit and the bravery she and Barak showed, the land entered a significant time of peace, lasting for over forty years. Listen to their song of praise and victory:

> *So may all your enemies perish, Lord! But may all who love you be like the sun when it rises in its strength.*
>
> — *Judges 5:31*

'Rising like the sun in its strength'—what a complete turnaround for the people of God! One day they were oppressed; the next they are entering their prime! And this is what seems to sit at the very core of the pioneering spirit: it leads to revival and reformation, breakthrough and change, the course of history being shifted in that time, that place, that season, that moment.

If pioneering sounds like a high and lofty ideal, a status only a few can obtain, I respond with an emphatic *No!* I believe that there are many areas God can call us to pioneer in. Deborah was a pioneer in being the first female judge of Israel; she was also pioneering as a prophet when she called and commanded the nation of Israel to go to war. As a judge, a prophet, a poet and a songwriter, Deborah was a multi-passionate and multi-gifted pioneer.

I want us to think about the word pioneering as it relates to our everyday lives. Not all of us will get opportunities to do things such as creating an invention or scaling a mountain. But I believe each of us, armoured up in the Lord with the two-edged sword of His Word in one hand and the shield of faith in the other, can take territory for the Lord. That territory may be a nation or community, a situation, an industry, a system, a method—anything that we can impact and influence for His Kingdom. Our ordinary lives in alignment with the Lord of heaven and earth can bring about the extraordinary.

A few years ago, I was introduced by a mutual friend to Steven Wamala, a young Ugandan pastor who founded the Barnabas Legacy Children's Dream Foundation (BLCDF), a childcare ministry to needy, orphaned children. Uganda is a country in East Africa of which forty-five percent of the population are children, and of those children, around twelve percent are orphans. Famine, constant conflict, AIDS, and poverty create many challenges. Nearly one out of every five children in Uganda is uneducated, and the rate is especially high for young girls living in rural areas. The 'Barnabas Foundation' provides protection, care, advocacy, and school holiday bible programmes, to over two hundred and fifty of these vulnerable children.

As I built a relationship with Steven and his team and got to know the children and understood the foundation's needs, God planted a desire within us to build a community school to which the BLCDF children could come, as well as other village children whose families could not afford the usual tuition fees. As a team we began planning, praying, and preparing. When a suitable piece of land was identified in 2021, I felt God tell me to pay for the purchase of this land. "Wow, Lord, did I hear you right?" I asked. My husband and I had a small bucket of savings which, after prayer and discussion together, we decided to sow into the purchase of this land. Then, just one week after we donated the money for the land, something totally unexpected happened. I received a bonus payment at work—exactly equal to the amount we had just sowed! I couldn't believe it! I hadn't even been in my new workplace for twelve months!

But God was on the move. During that year, I shared the vision for a school with friends and family across Australia and New Zealand. As a foundation board we wrote up a budget for building a kindergarten and primary campus, along with a list of the resources we thought would be needed. We set to prayer with a deep cry of, "Lord, You have called us to pioneer the work and we don't really know what we are doing, but with a mustard seed of faith we press in and we press on step by step. We are trusting in You with mountain-moving faith." I still had many a night when I woke up and thought, "Oh Lord, have we stepped out too much?" But God honoured our faith, and early the following year, a friend in New Zealand and her husband donated a significant sum of money as a memorial to her parents who had been missionaries to Ugandan orphans thirty years before! Only God could have orchestrated such provision. What an historic moment it was when the first brick was laid, and the building commenced!

Later in the year, Phase One of the building project was nearly finished, but further funds were required to ensure we could open the school for the first term of the upcoming year. As hubby and I prayed and thought on this, we sensed God leading us to draw on some of the equity in our house to sow into completing this phase. This involved extending our mortgage. "Oh Lord, is there another way?" we prayed. It didn't seem like a wise move, but God was urging us, and we stepped out in faith, knowing that pioneering is not for the weak or faint-hearted. Like Deborah, we'd heard a clear call, and like Deborah, we knew that call came at a cost, both figuratively and literally.

On contacting the bank, we filled in the paperwork and waited on a response. Three days later they called and said no, it wasn't possible for them to lend us the amount requested because the money would be going overseas. I remember putting the phone down and thinking, "Lord, I don't quite understand. I know we followed you, but maybe we didn't hear you right." The next morning, however, a different person called from the bank. He said he was ringing to let us know our money would be transferred that afternoon. All they needed was for us to sign the documents that were about to be emailed through to us. I was stunned—I said something along the lines of, "Yesterday we were told *no*. Why are we being told *yes* today?" He replied, "I have no idea why you were told no, but the answer is yes. There is no problem!"

I tell you this story because I want you to understand the varied ways and unique areas in which God calls each of us to pioneer. Some will be called to influence within an industry; for others it might be a nation or nations, while for others it could be their local parenting group. It is not about competing or comparing, but taking hold of that which He has given you to pioneer in. For us, it was a school in Uganda. Since then, new donors have come onboard, and are increasingly coming onboard in ways that amaze us. Today, the school opens its doors to one hundred and fifty students with the biggest smiles, and hearts hungry to learn. We are unsure of how the ongoing operational costs are going to be covered, or how God will provide funds so we can put in a playground. But what we are sure of is that He who calls us is faithful. He is a miracle working God, the same yesterday, today and forever. What God has done for me, He can do for you.

Cultivating a Pioneering Spirit

When God places a good work in our spirit, we can be confident that He will bring it to completion (Philippians 1:6). Even so, we need to partner with Him every step of the way, stretching out in faith and cultivating the pioneering spirit He has placed within each of us. Here are some ways we can do that:

Combine the Pioneering Spirit with the Prophetic Word

The call to pioneer, to be pioneering, begins in the hidden place. We need to receive a word, prophetic picture, or vision from God before we begin trailblazing. Moses knew the importance of this. When he was about to lead the people of Israel into the promised land, he prayed, "If your Presence does not go with us, do not send us up from here" (Exodus 33:15). He needed God's assurance that this was not just a 'good idea' but a 'God-idea'. That sort of clarity can come in many ways—through the scriptures, in prayer, or (as in my case) through a prophetic word. Just one year ago, I received a prophetic word about the school in Uganda:

> *Sons and daughters will arise out of this place; sons and daughters who will impact nations. Sons and daughters who will declare my word over the nations as Jeremiah did in his days. Sons and daughters who will carry a revival and a reformation anointing. Sons and daughters who will usher in the harvest fields. Sons and daughters who will preach my word and see souls saved, miracles happen, and the dead raised to life. Sons and daughters compelled by my love to serve and minister to a hurting and broken world. Sons and daughters who will have the healing balm of Gilead flowing in and through them; they will lay hands on the sick and they will be healed. Sons and daughters in this hour and for this hour.*

Dream and Dream Again

I know that our dreams can ebb away as life goes on, and the tough seasons we go through can discourage us from wanting to bring our dreams to the fore or to dream again in God. God was at work, weaving His Kingdom purposes into my heart long before I accepted Christ as my Saviour. In fact, ever since I was a young girl, even before I became a teacher, I dreamed of one day being able to build a school for children in poverty who would otherwise not be able to attend a school because they could not afford to pay the fees. Who would have known that God would resurrect that dream many years later? Yet that's what God does. He gives us dreams, and He helps us dream again!

So don't be discouraged. Think of the long-held dreams in your heart—perhaps dreams you have not told anyone but have been whispered only to the Father. I speak into your life today that the dreams of God will burst forth, explode, no longer just to be bubbling away, but that these dreams would be like a mighty volcano inside of you. Let's go forward, Mighty Deborahs, like Caleb who even at eighty years of age was saying, "Lord, give me this mountain" (Joshua 14:12).

Get Irritated

As pioneers, we are often led into new ventures by the things that irritate us. Is there a niche in the market no one seems to be meeting? Does your community lack the very thing you are looking for? There is a general principle that irritation leads to treasure. Think about how sand within an oyster leads to the formation of a pearl. When it comes to cultivating a pioneering spirit, think about the things that stir you, the situations that irk you or frustrate you, causing you to think, *If only they did it this way, with this method, with this process...* Then start praying and partnering with God as He brings solutions, ideas and strategies to His pioneering women!

Seek Solutions

Pioneers are solution seekers. I have worked in the business coaching and consulting field for many years, and one thing that has always frustrated me is how complicated starting a business has been made out to be, as though you have to have some superstar qualities and know every business principle inside out when you start. I believe self-employment or startup businesses are vehicles that everyone should be able to get a licence to drive. I feel there is a need to stop making business such a mystery, so unreachable. However, in working with clients in remote, rural and regional areas, I found women who encountered numerous barriers in starting a business, simply because of their location.

Flowing out of this frustration, about seven years ago I felt God prompt me to develop a business model that could assist women entrepreneurs in any location, and that worked equally well for product-based and service-based businesses. I called it the *5+U Pillars of Business Model* (see Appendix). As I developed this, God clearly showed me five distinct business 'pillars': Strategy, Legal Compliance, Marketing, Financial Matters, HR and Operations... and You, the business owner (hence 5+U)!

If you are looking for solutions to a problem or opportunity, be encouraged! Use the 5+U business tool, and step confidently into the unique area God has called you to pioneer.

Consider the Nations

One of my favourite scriptures is Psalm 2:8:

"Ask it of Me, and I will certainly give the nations as your inheritance, and the ends of the earth as your possession." (NASB)

Nations are on the heart of God. As you spend time in prayer and the Word, ask God for a nation or nations that He wants you to do pioneering work in. In what territory would He have you be an instrument for revival and reformation? Let Him reveal to you prophetic words to speak over that location. As God shows you the nation or nations, study about that region, learn about its people, begin to look at the news and the events happening there. Let your heart begin to break for those things which break His in that particular nation.

NATIONS, LORD, NATIONS!

"Ask of Me, I will give you the nations."
Lord, I ask of you: "Take me to the nations."
Let this heart be filled with compassion,
that I would move and speak with passion.

The soil of many nations is so hard and dry.
The rain of your Spirit needs to fall.
Break up the fallow ground,
That the nations would respond to the sound.

You place a trumpet in my hand,
and You bring it to my lips.
"Declare," You say, "declare":
Nations come near,
Nations come hear.

Your Word, O Lord, will thunder.
Your Word, O Lord, will flash as lightning.
Your Word, O Lord, will flood upon hearts.
Nations, nations, nations.

Stay in Faith

Pioneers are often people full of faith, but this doesn't mean an easy road! In most cases, pioneering involves opposition, so don't be surprised when you face it. We see in the book of Judges that when Barak was presented with the opportunity to take new ground, he became downcast to the point where he didn't even feel he had the strength to go on. Thankfully, mighty Deborah was there to speak into the situation and encourage his heart. As with Barak, the antidote to opposition and attack is to know your 'why'. It is your *why* that will drive you to your knees in challenging times and keep you praying and pressing into the Lord as you pioneer.

Believe for Your Tribe

My experience has been that as a pioneer you do go through quite significant periods of your journey by yourself. You have to be comfortable walking 'alone' but knowing you are never alone. The

Father draws near to those who draw near to Him. When Noah was building the ark, everyone was out and about enjoying the sunshine, with no concern for buying an umbrella or battening down the hatches. But on the day the rains came, it was Noah who was found ready with the solution—the boat! So, keep building your boat! Trust God to bring alongside those who will pioneer with you. When the time comes for the purpose to be revealed and activated, God will bring you to your tribe, those who will stand alongside you to build and pioneer in business, movement, and ministry.

REFLECTION QUESTIONS

1. What industry, place, people, situation or nation has God called you, as part of an 'army', to take possession of? Are there people on your heart who will return to what God has created them to be through what you pioneer?

2. The call to pioneer is not about self; it is about others. As pioneers we are freedom fighters, bringing the 'exiles' home. What is home to you? How could 'home' become more about your relationship with the Father?

3. Sit with the Father and ask Him to reveal to you more deeply the area, the method or the 'mountain' you are to pioneer. How might He want you to do that? Pour yourself into the scriptures and take note about what God is speaking to you about pioneering.

4. Is there an aspect of pioneering that makes you feel fearful or anxious, or makes you want to pull back from thinking of yourself as a pioneer? Journal your reflection and write a letter, poem or words to the Lord to help you step out of the fear and anxiety, or that which is holding you back.

CHAPTER FOUR

SHE IS VISIONARY

THE WRITER OF PROVERBS did not beat about the bush when it came to the topic of vision. In chapter 28 he wrote, "Without a vision, the people perish" (v 18). In Deborah's day, Israel was indeed perishing for lack of a vision. Thankfully, Deborah was a visionary leader.

To be visionary means to think about or plan for the future with imagination and wisdom. A 'visionary' has the ability to see what others do not yet grasp. God gave Deborah a vision of what Barak and the ten thousand men under his command were to do. As part of this vision, Deborah also saw that the Lord would not deliver Sisera, the enemy's commander, into the hands of Barak, but into the hands of a woman—Jael. To Deborah, what needed to be done seemed obvious, but Barak could not see what the future held. He struggled to understand what the Lord was doing. We read about this account in Judges 4:4-6.

> *She (Deborah) sent for Barak son of Abinoam from Kedesh in Naphtali and said to him, "The Lord, the God of Israel, commands you: 'Go, take with you ten thousand men of Naphtali and Zebulun and lead them up to Mount Tabor. I will lead Sisera, the commander of Jabin's army, with his chariots and his troops*

to the Kishon River and give him into your hands.'"

Barak said to her, "If you go with me, I will go; but if you don't go with me, I won't go."

"Certainly I will go with you," said Deborah. "But because of the course you are taking, the honour will not be yours, for the Lord will deliver Sisera into the hands of a woman."

It is easy to read these verses and picture Barak as weak and slow to react to what was going on. Yet, we have to pause here and remember that although Barak did not see the whole picture, he believed the vision Deborah shared. In faith, he gathered the ten thousand soldiers under his command. Ten thousand men is a large army! These men followed Barak into battle, and the battle was won.

If we are honest with ourselves, I think Barak is someone a lot of us can relate to. We think, *Lord, I am here, ready to do what you show me, but I can't quite see what it is I should do. I am feeling like maybe I might stuff this up, I feel weak and unsure.* In these 'Barak' moments, as we seek to outwork the vision God has given us, we need to meditate and lean into His Word. Some of my 'go to' biblical truths are:

- Our weaknesses are perfected in His strength (2 Corinthians 12:9)
- When we are weak, He is strong (2 Corinthians 12:10)
- He makes our feet like the feet of deer upon the mountain tops (Psalm 18:33)
- When our heart and flesh fail, He is the strength of our lives (Psalm 73:26)

Let's remember it is not our human efforts that will win battles; it is our trust and hope in the Lord. Be encouraged that despite his lack of vision, Barak was not ineffective in the task he was given to do. He simply acted in faith and obedience, trusting in the revelation he received through Deborah.

Deborah warned Barak that victory would come through a woman rather than through him, and that is precisely what happened. Deborah had a strong and clear vision. As a leader, she walked by faith, not by sight (2 Corinthians 5:7). Visionary leaders—both men and women—can step into the unknown trusting that, although they may not have the full plan or all the details, God will be faithful in what He has shown them.

To me, this demonstrates that leadership is more about vision than gender. I have been part of churches where women are honoured in their gifts, skills and talents, and if they happen to be gifted at teaching and leading, then they are given the opportunity to do that. I have also been in churches where the women are not considered for the roles of pastor, minister, preacher, or teacher. These churches focus on scriptures such as 1 Timothy 2:12: "I do not permit a woman to teach or to have authority over a man; she must be silent," and 1 Corinthians 14:34-35: "Women should remain silent in the churches. They are not allowed to speak, but must be in submission, as the law says. If they want to inquire about something, they should ask their own husbands at home; for it is disgraceful for a woman to speak in the church."

My personal view is that these scriptures must be read within the historical context rather than being used to determine what women can be permitted to do in today's world. At the time of Paul's writing, there was a lot of false teaching. The Ephesian women were caught up in this—they needed to learn truth, as they were speaking out falsehood. Just because the women in Ephesus were teaching falsely and needed to learn, however, does not mean women can't be good teachers and leaders elsewhere and in different times. The word 'silent' in Greek means to be calm or still—it does not mean you literally should not open your mouth or speak. God has created men and women to be complementary in skills and abilities, not for one gender to dominate the other. Yes, God is a God of gender equality! In Genesis 1:27 we read, "God created humankind in God's own image; in the image of God, God created them; male and female God created them." Likewise, in Galatians 2:26-28 Paul writes:

> *For in Jesus Christ you are all children of God through faith . . . there is neither Jew nor Greek, male nor female, slave nor free, for you are all one in Christ Jesus.*

Mighty Deborahs are visionary women who are called to take the lead in the areas which God has highlighted to them. They are to speak the 'commands' of the Lord. Whether you are chair on your local school council, or like myself, an advocate for the protection of children from all forms of abuse, or whether you are writing devotionals and bible studies, or setting up a business in a male-dominated industry, or a combination of all these things, it is not about gender; it is about *vision*.

Time and time again as I speak to women from all walks of life I am humbled to hear of their journey: the high tides and the low tides. As I listen, I begin to recognise the dreams deep within them, waiting to take flight, ready to see others be inspired, healed, uplifted and connected. The vision God has given me is to be a *Dream Nurturer: giving wings to magnificent dreams.* This is at the core of all I do across the suite of business ventures, projects, and ministry I put my hand to. I love to sit with women and hear their stories, their hopes and aspirations, and then walk alongside them to turn their dreams into reality and their adversity into success.

It is God who weaves the tapestry of His purposes and plans through our life story, and He ensures nothing in our lives is put to waste. As a girl, I was very shy and reserved, always too afraid to try something new or to make new friends. During my childhood, my siblings and I were never allowed to play with others or have friends around. We never went on school camps or excursions, and we rarely had family members visit us. Growing up as a young woman was not easy; I always had this sense of feeling marginalised and left out. I wasn't overly confident, and I didn't know how to interact well within groups of people. I felt like a bird trapped inside a cage, and I longed to break free and fly.

As a teenager, I spiralled into an emotional rollercoaster of anorexia, depression, and suicide attempts. It was only in my late teens, when friends encouraged me with their faith journeys that I started to find that personal faith path for myself. This strengthened me and helped me to make healthier choices for my life. My experiences as a girl and young woman created in me a strong desire to be a spokesperson for others in situations of injustice—to be a voice for girls and women who do not have a voice. My love for education led me to a teaching career and then into the fields of law and entrepreneurship. Teaching empowered me to find my voice, law empowered me to speak into situations of injustice, and being a businesswoman has enabled me to put on those wings and finally fly free—to get out of the cage and soar into the fullness and joy of what life has to offer.

As I have walked with the Lord through the years, He has placed in me deep passion and great compassion, along with a vision that propels me in every aspect of my personal, business and ministry life. That vision leads me to tap on the cages women find themselves in, ready to bind a broken wing, to breathe out fresh courage, to nudge a woman into flight in the power of her God, to ignite the gifts, talents, calling and skills that are deep within her being. In return, I ask of these women one thing—that as they leave imprisonment and begin flying freely, they would go and do the same for others—tapping on their cages so that their dreams can fly too.

God wants to expand our vision beyond ourselves. As modern-day Deborahs, we are called to lift one another up and enable others to find the currents and momentum to take them higher. Being visionary means that nothing is ever stagnant! God always has more to reveal to us! So don't become stuck in yesterday's vision but lean into the fresh manna of heaven each day. 1 Corinthians 2:9 tells us that God has prepared things that no eye has seen, no ear has heard, and no human mind has conceived for those who love him. I love this scripture. God always has more for us!

For me, founding the Deborah Conference was only the start. In 2019, God started to speak to me about this vision of creating a global community. The words I first wrote were, *"Come women, let us sit with Him and see what He says."* As I wrote these words, I saw a vision of a globe that was spinning on its axis. With each spin of the globe, a new nation stood out to me. And then, within those nations, I started to see towns and cities.

It was in my quiet times with the Lord over a period of months that He began to show me the vision for a prophetic company of harvest prayer warriors. I didn't understand every detail, but on one occasion as I was praying over what the Father was whispering to my heart, I saw the most beautiful trumpet. I opened the Word to Hosea 8:1 and read, "Put the trumpet to your lips."

As a result, the *Women Echo Him Collective* was birthed—a global community of women who 'put the trumpet to their lips,' prophetically praying and declaring God's heartbeat over towns, cities, and nations. The logo for the Collective is a trumpet, and I selected the acronym ECHO to explain the vision—that we are a community that:

Encourages hearts

Calls believers into the fullness of who they are in their Christ-given destiny and authority

Heralds (proclaims and declares) the messages of God over cities, nations and towns, and

Opens revelatory portals in the throne room of heaven so that many can ECHO the voice of God to their generation and to the generations to come.

This is why I am so passionate about calling Christian women entrepreneurs to awake and arise. As we nurture the visionary spirit God has placed in each of us, together we can shift the course of history!

CULTIVATING A VISIONARY SPIRIT

Here are some ways you can intentionally cultivate the vision God has placed within you:

Learn to Sit with the Lord

We are created for relationships. We get to know people best by spending quality time with them, by choosing to be present, undistracted by other things (such as mobile devices!). It is the same with our relationship with God. If we are to share His heart and receive vision from Him, we must slow down and learn to linger in His presence. This is not always easy. We live in a microwave society where everything, it seems, is instant. How convenient something is and how fast can it be delivered are two of the most important qualities in business.

I think we sometimes fall into the habit, albeit unintentionally, of desiring instant responses in our relationship with God. "Please, Lord, my time with You is short; please deliver what I am asking." Can I encourage you, as I encourage myself, to spend quality time with the Lord. Enjoy the macro-moments and the micro-moments. I know life can be very full and busy, but our relationship with God needs to be nurtured and built. Set aside time with God to allow Him to speak and show you His heart, His visions, and His plans.

I remember a picture God once gave me. It was of heavenly filing cabinets. Surrounding the filing cabinets were swirls of amazing light—His glory. The filing cabinets were of different sizes and colours. Some cabinets had open drawers, and inside were thick files and scrolls. I asked the Lord what this meant. I felt God say to me, "These are the heavenly filing cabinets filled with the projects, assignments, visions and tasks I have for my people." I said to the Lord, "Why are the cabinets so full?" He replied, "Because My people have not sought Me for vision—they look at the filing cabinet but do not open it. I go to give them a scroll but they don't stay long enough for Me to explain the details." It was a powerful invitation—one I extend to you today. Reader, come sit with the Lord and see what He will show you.

Serve Another Person's Vision for Awhile

Our journey in God is about growing in maturity in Christ, of transitioning from a 'milk diet' to a 'meat diet' as it were (1 Peter 2:2). This maturity process often takes place, not so much in outworking our own vision, but in serving another person's vision.

My encouragement to you is this: don't rush the plans and purposes of God! When God starts to speak and show you what He has purposed and planned for you, tread slowly. Be content to sit and listen before you hurry out and get started. Hunger to learn, grow and understand—just as Jesus did in the years leading up to His public ministry when, according to Luke 2:52, He "increased in wisdom and stature, and in favour with God and man."

One way to grow and learn is to serve another person's vision for a period of time. For example, if you want to go into business, offer to volunteer with a business owner you admire. Support them and their business in any way you can—even if just for a few hours each week. Or if you feel that God is giving you a vision to build and lead a youth group but there are no openings for leadership, serve in another ministry where you can learn leadership principles. Luke 16:12 (NLT) gives us this principle when it says, "If you are not faithful with other people's things, why should you be trusted with things of your own?"

Get Mentors and Coaches

Every God-given vision includes many aspects that need to be outworked. At times, despite our enthusiasm, it can become wearisome moving through the project, tasks or assignments that God has given to us. When this happens, we don't need to fear something is wrong; it is a reminder of our human nature! I love the passage in Exodus 17:12-14 where Moses is supported on either side by Aaron and Hur. Moses wore the mantle to lead the children of Israel through the battle, but he needed to be surrounded by those who could support him and lift him up. So, for encouragement's sake, I urge you to consider finding a mentor to support you in the vision and projects the Lord has entrusted to you.

A mentor is also helpful for accountability. Although I have written prolifically over the years and have published e-books, I had a mentor to help me get this book written. In our sessions together, my writing mentor drew 'gold' out of me, gold that I did not know I had. The questions she skilfully asked helped me consider the content I wanted to include and decide how to shape my chapters. A mentor or coach is there to help you run your God-given race well, to ensure you are found not only at the start line, keen, eager and willing—as many of us are—but at the finishing line too, where you will hear our Father say, "Well done, good and faithful daughter" (Matthew 25:23).

Make a Start

As with anything in life, the hardest part, don't you find, is actually starting? We can end up having talkfests for years, or rummaging around and around with our thoughts, or filling up notebooks and journals of this thing or that thing which we intend to do. Can I strongly encourage you to simply start? Stop reading this book right now and spend fifteen minutes taking a micro-step towards a vision God has given you. Perhaps God is pressing on your heart the idea of creating a line of homewares with scriptures on them so that people's homes become filled with the Word of God. In fifteen minutes you could write down three scriptures that you will use on your first line of homeware, and consider why you have chosen them. As you take those starting steps, remember, the steps of a good man (or woman) are ordered by the Lord (Psalm 37:23)!

Be Gentle on Yourself

The rhythm of life that we all experience includes both good moments and bad—the ebbs and the flows. Sometimes it can feel like the tide is fully in and there is movement, satisfaction, and feelings of achievement and fulfilment. In another season, the tide may be well out. Even visionaries can become weary. When hope ebbs, or you feel broken and bruised, you might even wonder if the Lord will ever use you again. At times like this, it is difficult to see what might be ahead, just over the horizon.

This is a poem I wrote at a time when I was feeling broken and discouraged. I was navigating the grief of not being able to be a biological mother, and I no longer felt like a visionary; in fact, I was unable to think about or plan for the future. My prayer is that this poem will encourage you to know that you *will* dance once again, and your 'vision' *will* return.

I WILL DANCE ONCE AGAIN

I will sing aloud of His faithfulness to me.
In the darkest hour, His love still held me
I lay on my bed broken to the core.
Yet each piece of my humanity He bore
Upon the cross of Calvary.

My pain and hurt He took,
The nails that pierced His hands and feet,
The blood that flowed was for me.
I lift my head to see Him there.
The song in my heart I begin to hear.

I look not at the brokenness, but to the Cross
Where I see wholeness.

He gently pulls me back up on my feet.
Lifts the curtains of grief off my heart.
We pause a while in the shade,
Until infused by Him I can now dance once again.

Embrace Your Womanhood

Finally, I want to exhort you, don't let your 'gender' become a stumbling block, an excuse not to stir up the gifts of God within you. I have experienced, at times, my gender being used as a barrier against me. "Surely, Maree you can't do that, because God wouldn't have women do that or go here or there." But our assurance and our validation do not come from others; they come from our God. Yes, we need to have wise counsel around us—we are not meant to do life alone—but we must determine not to let naysayers, religious folk, and toxic people (some of whom can sometimes be family members) pull us back. Surround yourself with cheerleaders and champions, those who spur you on to all that God has in you, and for you. Reader, we are history-makers! Now, go and make history, for the sake of His Kingdom purposes in this hour!

Reflection Questions

1. What vision has God given you for your business? If you are stuck on how to write a vision statement for your business, try filling in this sentence: "My vision is to _____ so that _____". For example, the vision statement for my online coaching practice is "To *help mid-life professional women turn their expertise and experiences into a sustainable business* so that *they can make an impact and leave a legacy, creating a ripple effect.*"

2. Now do the same for the vision God has given you for your personal life or ministry life. My vision statement for my personal life is: To *inspire women (young and old) to give wings to their magnificent dreams* so that *they can fly free and, in turn, inspire others, creating a ripple effect.*

3. Consider two barriers that hold you back from the vision, assignments and projects God has given you. Perhaps it is fear, or the need to navigate family responsibilities. Ask the Lord to help you find ways to break through these barriers. Brainstorm some ideas with a friend or mentor.

4. Share your vision statements with a trusted friend and ask them to pray that God would continue to show you how to outwork the vision He has given you.

CHAPTER FIVE

SHE IS MOTHERING

THERE ARE MANY WORDS which could be used to describe Deborah—words like judge, prophetess, deliverer, intercessor, or worshipper. However, the word Deborah chose to describe herself is 'mother'. This is interesting, as the book of Judges doesn't tell us who her children were. The phrase, "I arose, a mother in Israel" in Judges 5:7 can mean that she was a mother 'in Israel' or that she was a mother 'over Israel'. Either way, her heart was for the children of Israel—literally and figuratively. And although we do not know for certain whether Deborah was a mother of her own biological children, we do see in the scripture that God's people looked to her for leadership and authority as the nation's mother (Judges 5:6-7).

Deborah's Compassion

Among the many characteristics Deborah displayed of a good mother, the quality that stands out to me most is her compassion. Deborah's heart ached when she saw Israel in distress, wandering without a purpose, and turning away from God. Her heart was moved when the children of Israel were in strife. This reminds me of Jesus' reaction to the crowds in Matthew 9:36: "When He saw the crowds, He had compassion on them, because they were harassed and helpless, like sheep without a shepherd."

As modern-day Deborahs we should pay attention to the things (or people) that move our hearts. What happens inside you when you see a certain person, situation, place, nation or people-group harassed and helpless? To be mothering is to be compassionate.

Deborah's Wisdom

Another quality of mothering we see in Deborah's life is her wisdom. Judges 4:5 tells us that many came to her to "have their disputes decided." Deborah gave wise judgement. Think of a mum you know, especially one who has more than one child. There are many moments when that mum will have to solve disputes, settle arguments between the children, exude wisdom in her decisions, help her children with understanding life's lessons, and restore peace in the home. Deborah's home was Israel, and God had positioned her to be a mother to Israel—settling their arguments, problem-solving, giving direction (Barak, go!), always seeking to bring about peace and restore Israel's heart to God. No easy feat!

Deborah's Integrity

To be mothering is to lead those whom God has given you to mother; to raise them up; to be kind, caring and protective, but firm and fair—just a like a mama bear with her cubs. Deborah's heart was with Israel's princes, the next generation coming through.

In Judges 5:9-10 we hear her words:

> *My heart is with Israel's princes, with the willing volunteers among the people. Praise the Lord! You who ride on white donkeys,*

sitting on your saddle or blankets, and you who walk along the road, consider . . .

Mothers keep a particular watch over the young ones because they are aware that in the years to come, the princes will be kings and the princesses will be queens; the leaders of the next generation. But mothers are not prepared to simply go along with the status quo—they are truth-tellers and call out what is wrong, and what needs to be reflected and considered. Deborah called out to those whose 'luxurious' standard of living—the white donkeys and saddle blankets—had become such a way of life that it was causing them to turn away from the Lord. She challenged these ones: "As you walk along the road, consider." In much the same way, the Lord exhorted His people in Haggai 1:7 saying, "Give careful thought to your ways."

Deborah's Teaching

Part of the revelation God gave me from the life of Deborah is that an important aspect of mothering is to be a teacher. Deborah taught her 'children' about what happened in times past, both the good and the bad, and the lessons that could be gained and gleaned. She told the children of Israel, "Look, this is what our God did, and when God moved the earth shook, the rains came, the mountain quaked, before the Lord, the God of Israel" (Judges 5:4-5) In so doing, Deborah taught Israel who their God was and who He had called them to be.

What a powerful lesson! Children are always rushing for what is ahead. How many times does a child ask you when their next birthday will be, or when Christmas is coming. When we are adults, it's the opposite—we often exclaim that we want time to stop going so fast! The past shapes the future, and Deborah wanted to make sure the people of God were educated about their history in God.

~

I have always had a strong desire to be a mother. My family home was one with limited celebrations or times of joy. I often felt a lot of sadness. We had food, clothing, a roof over our heads and an education, but there were large pockets of emotional neglect. As a girl, one thing I always dreamed of was throwing birthday parties for my future children, or taking them to the circus, or surprising them with wonderful adventures.

I didn't meet my husband until I was thirty-nine, but we got married within a year of meeting each other—when God moves, He moves! My husband is a beautiful Fijian chief who shared my desire to have children. We got pregnant three times over a period of two years, but each time I lost the baby in utero within the first two months. This season of our life was indescribably hard, and I filled my tear bottles in heaven many times over. God did not forget our pain, however. Over time, my dream of having biological children became a seed that died. But I have seen the truth of John 12:24 in my own life: "Very truly I tell you, unless a kernel of wheat falls to the ground and dies, it remains only a single seed. But if it dies, it produces many seeds." The single seed of my desire which died has certainly become many seeds.

I do realise, however, that for many women, accepting this will be an ongoing challenge. Mothering—however that looks—can be a sensitive topic. Some women face painful infertility, and others struggle with societal expectations of the 'right' way to be a mum. There is always ongoing pressure, and we put more than enough pressure on ourselves as well. Even so, God has created women to be mothering, and we should wear this mantle confidently, unafraid and unperturbed by what the world might say to us or about us.

This doesn't mean we always *feel* motherly. When a baby is placed in my arms, of course it is beautiful to goo and gah and celebrate that little life. But if I am very honest (and brave!)—and I want to be because I think some readers will resonate with this—I don't always *feel* motherly when a bub is passed to me. I don't always *feel* motherly when I help at children's church, I don't always *feel* motherly when a friend asks me to child-mind for an evening. But I am *mothering*—caring, compassionate, protective, wise, a leader, speaker, and teacher. And so are you! You have been given a mothering spirit in whatever sphere of life God has positioned and anointed you.

Over the years, both prior to being married and after, God regularly had people speak a particular prophetic encouragement over my life—that I would be like Sarah, a mother of many nations. We find God's promise to Sarah in Genesis 17:16:

> *I will bless her and will surely give you a son by her. I will bless her so that she will be the mother of nations; kings of peoples will come from her.*

This verse always kept me pressing into God for what I thought was to be my own biological children—but it wasn't to be that way. My heart's cry became, "God, You work all things together for good to those who love You and who have been called according to His purpose."

I was a child protection lawyer and trainer for several years. After I lost our second baby earthside, I really struggled to do the child protection training. I felt like such a fraud—here I was teaching others about the signs and symptoms of child abuse and neglect, championing the protection of children, and I couldn't even carry any of my own. One week while running a course we had a guest speaker who was a very experienced paediatrician. During question time at the end of her session, one of the participants said to her she must be an amazing mother because of her vast knowledge of children's needs and how to care for them. She replied: "I am not a mother; I haven't been able to have children, but I adore being an aunty and I love the work I do."

Afterwards, I apologised to the speaker for the participant's question and shared with her my own heartache. Her reply became a turning point for me. "Maree, if you were going for heart surgery, would you rather be operated on by a heart surgeon or by someone who has been through heart surgery?" Of course, I replied, "By the heart surgeon." The reflection for me was you don't have to be a biological mother to be motherly.

Of course, the pain of not bearing my own children—pain I know some of you may relate to—is not easy. At times I find my desire to be a mother pulling strongly on my heartstrings. As I have continued to journey in the Lord, His peace and His healing have strengthened me to the point where I have finally given myself permission to *be mothering* and not inwardly resist when people say things like, "You are such a Mama Bear, you are always caring and kind and looking out for others." This happens often in workplaces where I have been the leader, manager or teacher; my team members would often say, "Oh, we will just ask Mama Bear what to do." I am not always comfortable being named that, but I have come to see it as an endearing term of affection.

I have had the privilege of being part of many women's lives. They are spread out across many nations and now I see many with 'cubs' of their own—both biological and figurative—that they are raising.

The 'Sarah' word over my life has come (and is still coming) true! In the village where we established the school in Africa, older women are called mamas regardless of whether they have their own children. The name given to me by the team, the local women and the children is 'Mama Queen'. My husband's Fijian community have also taken to calling me the Fijian term for older women, *Nau*, which means grandmother. I am called this regularly; even my husband uses the term to refer to me. It took some time to get used to, as it had always been an 'ouch' point, but slowly God has worked His healing in me.

How precious, how divine, how cool is our God! Not one word of God's promises will fail (Joshua 21:45)—not *one word*. You know what, Mighty Deborah? I can say without a doubt, "God knows! God works! God restores!" He is the God of the yes and amen. He has made me a "mother of many nations."

CULTIVATING A MOTHERING SPIRIT

The story of Deborah offers several clear lessons on how to cultivate a mothering spirit in our own lives. Deborah was a mother to the nation of Israel, but the application points below can be applied in any context, whether parenting your own child, or mothering other people, a team, a nation, a church, or a community.

Cultivate Strong Emotional Intelligence

Deborah was a kind, caring, protective and compassionate woman with a lot of patience. Holding court like she did, day in and day out, she needed to keep an open mind and a soft heart if she was to reach firm and equitable decisions. She was a woman who needed to listen intently to each party's side of the story and see 'beneath the surface'.

Emotional intelligence (EQ) is the ability to identify and regulate your own emotions, as well as being able to understand the emotions of others. A high EQ helps reduce stress, defuse conflict, and build relationships. Someone with high EQ is a person you would describe as warm, engaging, and personable. I see these qualities in Deborah; she was a leader with great authority, but she led with her head *and* her heart—the heart representing emotional intelligence. Let's be women who tune in to the emotional needs of others and take the time to look below the surface, to perceive and honour the heart matters that others may overlook.

Cultivate Wisdom

Proverbs 4:7 tells us that wisdom is the most important thing we can have, and we should spend our all in seeking it. In Deborah's role as judge and prophet she needed to be very wise—wise with her words, wise in her decisions, wise in her timing, and wise in her commands. I encourage you to study the scriptures on wisdom and ask the Lord to give you more wisdom. How often do you hear yourself saying, "Where has common sense gone these days?!" I know I say it a lot! But we know that if anyone lacks wisdom, we can ask the Lord and He will give it generously and liberally (James 1:5). Wisdom will enable you to act with good judgement, using your knowledge, understanding, experiences, insights, and common sense. Just as Solomon asked for wisdom in order to be a better leader of his people (2 Chronicles 1:11-12), we too should ask the Lord for wisdom and trust that He will give it to us lavishly.

Cultivate Your Leadership Skills

To be mothering is to lead, to be a leader. There are of course, different levels and layers of leadership. For many women, being a leader to their own children is the focus. Others may lead as a CEO in a business, as a chair on a board, as principal of a school, as president of a nation, as a pastor of a church, or any combination thereof. Each type of leadership involves honing different skills and knowledge. One way to intentionally hone your skills is to read and listen to good content about leadership.

The second way to cultivate leadership skills is to learn to serve. Godly leaders find their role model in Jesus. The scriptures tell us: "Even the Son of Man did not come to be served, but to serve, and to give his life as a ransom for many" (Mark 10:45). A godly leader not only serves those being led but knows that there is self-sacrifice; there is a cost involved. For Jesus, that sacrifice led to His death on the cross; for Deborah, she had to go out to the battlefield with Barak instead of staying under the palm tree in her 'comfort zone'. Mothering, however it looks, requires this kind of servant leadership.

Cultivate Your Speaking Skills

Mothering involves speaking to those who follow you. Speaking is not something that came naturally to me as a young adult because I was never given the opportunity to voice my opinions or thoughts and was used to living in silence. Thank God for His grace and healing which has brought me to a place where I am able to speak up and speak out. I am now able to speak in situations where I know my knowledge, experience and insight is helpful and valued, and to speak out for those in challenging situations—to be an advocate for them.

We hone our speaking skills by using them. Speaking doesn't have to be something as big as preaching a sermon from the church pulpit (though it can be). It can also be sharing in your local Mums and Bubs group, or at a board meeting. Speaking might involve advocating for a people-group or for those facing injustice. Over the years, I have developed specialist skills and knowledge in the area of trauma. As I have intentionally grown in this area, I have begun to use a trauma-informed lens across all the business and community endeavours I am involved in. I speak up and speak out about trauma's impact and how to navigate its trails. When God places on our hearts specific things to speak about, it is our task to begin to do just that. Mothering involves speaking for those who can't, and speaking to teach those who are your children—whether literally, or of the heart.

Cultivate Your Teaching Skills

As a judge and prophet, Deborah would have been involved in many 'teachable moments' as she handed down judgements, explaining what was right or wrong, and what the consequences of those wrongdoings should be. As a prophet she taught the people about the Lord and what He was going to do. There are different layers and levels of teaching skills, and each of us is gifted differently. Not everyone will become a secondary school teacher or preach in church, but we can all create teachable moments, share life lessons, and impart the scriptures to those the Lord has given us to 'mother'.

Deuteronomy 6:7-9 (NIrV) tells us to teach the things of the Lord diligently:

> *The commandments I give you today must be in your hearts. Make sure your children learn them. Talk about them when you are at home. Talk about them when you walk along the road. Speak about them when you go to bed. And speak about them when you get up. Write them down and tie them on your hands as a reminder. Also tie them on your foreheads. Write them on the doorframes of your houses. Also write them on your gates.*

I also love Romans 10:14: "But how can they call on him to save them unless they believe in him? And how can they believe in him if they have never heard about him? And how can they hear about him unless someone tells them?" (NLT). As mothers, we get to tell the story and message of Jesus. So, let's rise up and speak! If we do not tell or teach those God brings our way, how will they know who Jesus is and what He has done?

Reflection Questions

1. What person, situation, or people-group do you most feel compassion for?

2. What characteristic of mothering would you like to dive deeper into? Study some scriptures about this characteristic and read or listen to resources on the subject.

3. Get together with two or three friends and talk about the topic of mothering. Glean from one another about how God uses each of you in this area. Which sensitivities, or 'ouch' points around 'mothering' could you pray about together?

4. Think of a young person and send a card encouraging them in who they are, their gifts, abilities, and who God is and wants to be in their life. You might like to remind them of Jeremiah 29:11: "For I know the plans I have for you," declares the LORD, "plans to prosper you and not to harm you, plans to give you hope and a future."

PART TWO
ARISE

CHAPTER SIX

SHE IS SKILFUL

DESPITE THE CHALLENGES OF getting to her position, Deborah chose to use the skills and gifts that God had given her. She understood that preparation and training were integral to what she was doing; she was a skilled woman.

When God calls us to a position of influence, as He did with Deborah, He will take us on a journey of skill-building, readying us for the task at hand. It is God who opens the doors—no amount of pushing from us can open them! Proverbs 18:16 says, "A man's gifts will make room for him" (NKJV). It is walking in authenticity and integrity with a heart that is fully surrendered to the Father that will cause others to recognise your skills and talents. So keep living your life before God one day at a time, one step at a time, walking in obedience to what He is telling you to do next, cultivating and using your skills as you go.

Deborah's skillset was certainly impressive! Her resume included roles as warrior, poet, prophet, singer, and songwriter. But predominantly, Deborah's 'job' was judging the people of Israel. Becoming a judge is not something that just happens overnight. It is a difficult and challenging position—one that comes with a lot of responsibility and the weight of knowing that you are making decisions that will impact people's lives. Deborah was most likely selected because she was faithful in doing what God had 'put in her hand'; she was already using the skills and talents that God had given her. Even so, Deborah most likely had a period of preparation and training for the role.

It concerns me when people dismiss gaining qualifications as a way of fulfilling what God has called us to do. In Christian culture there has sometimes been the suggestion that tertiary qualifications are 'worldly' and do not really matter because it is God who appoints and equips a person for a certain position or role. Of course, this is true—God does call us and position us—but many of the roles He calls us to require some level of training or expertise if we are to fulfil them with excellence. God is delighted when we sharpen, hone, and practise the skills and talents He has given us, and often this is done through engaging in different forms of training and qualifications.

What has been your experience with formal training or education? Perhaps you have been dismissed by others or told by people that getting qualified (for instance, obtaining a degree) was merely a phase in your life and there was probably something better you could have done in place of going to university. That is simply not true. Deborah was a judge, not simply because she wanted to be one. No, she would have had to exhibit the required qualities, demonstrate her abilities, and work at improving them. In today's world, she would have had to go through extensive training to get qualified and then worked under supervision as a lawyer before being admitted to the bar. You don't simply jump from wanting to be a judge to being one the next minute.

If you carry hurt or discouragement in your heart in this area of your life, may I encourage you to lift that hurt up to the Father right now. Allow Him to bathe your wound. He is the healing balm of Gilead (Jeremiah 8:22), and remember, what the enemy intended for evil, your God will work for good (Genesis 50:20). It's never too late to formally pursue the calling on your life.

When I started my first degree, I did not have in my heart that I was called to be a teacher. I simply stepped out in faith and did what I sensed God directing me to do—trusting that as I took those first steps, He would reveal the next steps to take after that. First, I went to university where I studied accounting and economics. I chose a commerce degree because I had felt God stirring my heart to increase my understanding of policy, economic systems, and the use of numbers. Then, after I finished my commerce degree, I went to Teachers College and obtained a diploma in secondary school teaching. Even then I did not truly believe I could be a teacher. I felt so uncomfortable in those first few months as I sat in my classes learning about and practising teaching—I was still very shy and reserved. I wasn't known for being in a crowd, let alone speaking at the front of one! At times, simply speaking in a small group was nerve-wracking.

Walking out our calling from God with the skills and talents He has given us doesn't mean it will be a comfortable ride. Think about the children of Israel crossing over into the promised land. Yes, they had just miraculously come through the Red Sea and out of bondage and slavery in Egypt and yes, the promised land was right in front of them, but (there is that *but* word again!) in order to take hold of the land they had to go into a daunting time (in their case, a time of battle).

When I stepped into Teachers College, it seemed on the surface—and I certainly felt—that I did not have the skills or aptitude to be a teacher. Even my family and friends were surprised by my decision to undertake that training course. Yet in my spirit I knew this was the next step I was to take. It is a hard feeling to articulate. It is that place in your relationship with God where deep calls unto deep (Psalm 42:7). It is knowing that He is drawing you, calling you, showing you what to do. In the natural, what is being asked of you may seem counterintuitive, but in the spiritual, it is the perfect fit. In the words of Proverbs 16:9, we may plan our way, but it is the Lord who directs our steps. Amazingly, it was teaching that ultimately helped me find my voice and learn to use it confidently in the strength and power of my heavenly Father.

For me, teaching was not the final destination. In my mid-thirties, I began to feel a pull on my heart to move in the direction of law, to learn how to negotiate and diffuse conflict, and how to bring ideas and solutions to unjust situations. I sensed God was growing a burden in me for His justice as scriptures like Micah 6:8, "Do justice, love mercy and walk humbly with God," began to capture my attention.

I went back to university and began a law degree. As with my first degree and teaching diploma, at the time I did not fully know what God wanted me to do within the area of law, but I focussed on learning and growing my skills. In some of my subjects, students I had taught in high school were now my fellow classmates, so it was an interesting transition to now be a student alongside them! I found, however, that I had an aptitude for the law—something I didn't know I had until I started. I felt almost guilty that I took to it so easily!

Daniel 1:17 tells us that God gave Daniel, Shadrach, Meshach and Abednego knowledge and understanding of all kinds of literature and learning. This is often what happens when we pursue our gifting. As I was meditating on this verse, I felt God showing me that I was learning legal principles and how the law operates so I could have more impact in areas of justice, especially areas of social justice like the distribution of wealth, and opportunities and privilege in society. He was giving me knowledge and understanding in order to do His work.

I also discovered that my other legal passion was family law and child protection. Getting my law degree (and then my master's) was not about chasing further letters after my name—something I was often teased about, which pained me—nor was it about the qualifications per se. It was about being faithful with what God had called me to, and trusting Him as He took me through the process of building the skills required for His mission for me.

CULTIVATING YOUR SKILLSET

When we feel that strong tug of God's call on our life, we often want to jump straight into it. Our hearts burst with excitement and anticipation, our minds start racing, and our heart's cry is, "Yes, Lord, let's go and do this!" We want to go from Step One to Step Ten in an instant. It is much like when a child learns to ride a bike for the first time. They eagerly jump on the bike and attempt to take off, but they have not yet mastered how to use the pedals, how to steer, and how to apply the brakes. God does not want to squash our enthusiasm or diminish our surrender to His call. Remember, we are children of God! He loves that we are so eager and keen. But (there's that word again!) outworking the call of God on our lives is not a cookie-cutter exercise or a series of microwave moments. It takes deliberate cultivation of the skills we will need.

Practise and Learn

Skills are mostly developed through practise—as the saying goes, practise makes perfect! If you feel God nudging you to increase your skills in a particular area, go and find the resources, the podcasts, the books, the YouTube clips, the mentors and the courses that will enable you to sharpen and hone those skills. Remember, there are many avenues through which you can learn and there are different ways of learning. For example, I am an avid reader, so my learning style is visual—give me words, diagrams, models, illustrations etc., and I am in my happy place. My husband is more of a kinaesthetic learner, so he builds skills best when he is doing things and engaged in immersive, experiential, and hands-on learning. Thus, some of us may enrol in a tertiary course, while others might choose to hone their skills through monthly practical sessions with a mentor.

It may be that you are an artist and God wants you to develop your skills as an art entrepreneur, commercialising your artwork. Or perhaps you are a policy writer and God is speaking to you about gaining a deeper understanding of how to write policy that does not merely sit in a hard drive somewhere but is practical and effective in the workplace or organisation you are placed in. This is where faith needs to be combined with action. Action builds momentum—faith without works is dead (James 2:14). Write down a list of ideas of how you can grow the skills and abilities you have; that which God has put in your heart to do. It is never too late to learn new skills.

Seek Healing and Freedom

Through my teaching and law careers, God revealed more and more to me about how trauma keeps people trapped. It is almost like an intersection, with despair and inaction on one side, hope and action on the other, and trauma sitting in the middle. Over the past few years, I have been intentionally seeking a deeper understanding of trauma. I sought out specialists in the field, read their books, listened to their podcasts, took their courses. Then, at fifty-five years of age, God opened a door for me to do my PhD on a subject close to my heart: "Business as a Trauma Recovery Tool for First Nations Women." I admit I find my brain does not quite work as fast or efficiently as it once did, which frustrates me at times. I often find myself asking, "God, do You really think I can do this?" He gently challenges me, "Yes, you can." And so I will seek to be faithful in sharpening and honing the skills that God has given me. I know that this will enhance the way I work with clients, communities and organisations who need a trauma-responsive approach.

I particularly want to encourage those of you who are currently completing, or considering further qualifications and training, even totally changing the career path you have had because you feel the Lord's hand guiding you to it. Perhaps you are sensing opposition—and it is from those close to you; you can feel that they are rolling their eyes at you. You know they are not consciously trying to pull you down or put you off, but you can't help but feel the sting of hurt. Let me reassure you, no matter the reactions you get from others, your further qualifications and training, and those letters after your name, are not ungodly or a waste of time. If you intentionally pursue God's guiding, you will go from strength to strength. Do not dismiss what God is speaking over you.

I also challenge you, don't be tempted to think that because God has called you to something and given you the required skills and talents, you don't need to practise, hone, and gain experience in different fields and in different seasons. How did David learn to fight Goliath? He first learned how to wield a sling as he fought off lions and bears among the rolling hills and fields as shepherd boy. David was considered lesser than his brothers, yet all along he was being honed for the task of delivering God's people. So keep training and you will grow in confidence in the sphere God has for you.

Know Your Uniqueness

I want to encourage you that your skills and talents do not have to look like everyone else's. Focusing our time and efforts on comparing ourselves to others is not the way to go. Psalm 139 tells us we are fearfully and wonderfully made. God saw you being knitted together in your mother's womb and your days were laid out in His book before you were born.

Let us look at Jael for a moment. Judges 5:24 says she was "the most blessed of tent-dwelling women." Having spent five years living in a very remote part of North-west Australia, I have come to appreciate the skills this woman needed! Let me tell you, I had to rapidly acquire the ability to survive in the bush—from dealing with snakes and crocodiles to navigating roads without phone reception, being cut off from food supplies due to flooding, off-road driving on corrugated, dusty tracks, plus actually learning how to put up a tent and hammer tent pegs in! You really must have your wits about you, and you need to be resilient, resourceful and capable at what you are doing! Certainly, Jael was capable. We read:

> *He asked for water, and she [Jael] gave him milk; in a bowl fit for nobles, she brought him curdled milk. Her hand reached for the tent peg, her right hand for the workman's hammer. She struck Sisera, she crushed his head, she shattered and pierced his temple. At her feet he sank, he fell; there he lay. At her feet he sank, he fell; where he sank, there he fell—dead. (vv. 25-27)*

Judges 5:24-27 is not the most palatable scripture to read, but what I want us to glean from these scriptures is that Jael had the skills necessary to carry out her God-given assignment, to defeat the

SHE IS SKILFUL

enemy by driving a tent peg through his head. Practically, that is not an easy thing to do—you certainly would need to know what you were doing!

I know not all of us, me included, would rejoice at being given an assignment such as Jael's, but she was bold and courageous in her God and did not shy away from using her skills to do what He had led her to. She did not dismiss the call and say, "Excuse me, God, you have the wrong person here. Want to give this job to someone else?" or "Excuse me, God, have you not noticed that I am a woman? A woman killing a man using a tent peg and a hammer is not the usual way of stopping an enemy!"

But like Deborah, Jael was a woman who had great impact on the course of Israel's history. Likewise, God is preparing, equipping and training you for the time we are in. He has positioned you, and will continue to position you, for a significant assignment to outwork among the nations. Mighty Deborahs, you are called to impact nations through the skills and talents He has given you!

Reflection Questions

1. What skills, training and preparation do you need or are you currently gaining in order to walk in what God has called you to do? Don't despise the day of small things—for the Lord rejoices to see the work begin! (Zechariah 4:10)

2. Are you using the skills God has already given you? How are you putting what He has birthed in you into action?

3. What skills are you sensing God wants to sharpen and hone further, and in what way?

4. Who is a mentor you could reach out to in your business, industry, or area of specialisation? Book in some sessions with them to learn and glean from them.

CHAPTER SEVEN

SHE IS STRATEGIC

BEING STRATEGIC TAKES A lot of guts! Courage is needed to lead people into something that is uncertain or that has not been done before. Deborah was more than just a strategist—she was a *military* strategist! But she did not come up with the strategy alone. God gave her a battle plan to pass on to Barak. Consequently, Barak and his army were in the right place at the right time, not of their own doing, but because God used Deborah to give the direction and tactics. As a result of her military strategy, the enemy was defeated. Sisera, the commander, came with nine hundred chariots, but they fled on foot. Judges 4:11,16 tell us what happened:

> *Then Deborah said to Barak, "Go! This is the day the Lord has given Sisera into your hands. Has not the Lord gone ahead of you?" So Barak went down Mount Tabor, with ten thousand men following him. At Barak's advance, the Lord routed Sisera and all his chariots and army by the sword, and Sisera got down from his chariot and fled on foot. Barak pursued the chariots and army as far as Harosheth Haggoyim, and all Sisera's troops fell by the sword; not a man was left.*

Not one man was left! What a testimony to heavenly strategies outworked through God's people. When God moves, God moves! Anointed strategy is what causes mountains to fall and the plans of the enemy to come to naught.

The scriptures contain other instances of such military strategy being given by God. In Deuteronomy 28:7 we read, "The LORD will grant that the enemies who rise up against you will be defeated before you. They will come at you from one direction but flee from you in seven." Exodus 15:3 says, "The Lord is a warrior: the Lord is his name."

God fights for His people even today. He wants to wipe out the enemies in your life—unhealthy character traits, pain and sorrow that keeps you bound, situations that keep you blinded and defeated. As Mighty Deborahs we must seek God for the 'military' strategy to rout out our 'enemies'. But strategists are also involved in planning and directing military movements in a war or battle, and Barak knew he needed Deborah, a military strategist, at his side. In fact, he said to Deborah, "If you go with me, I will go; but if you don't go with me, I won't go." (Judges 4:8).

What do you think Barak would have been thinking? "Deborah, like heck are you telling me what to do, and where to go, with whom; are you sure about all of this?" We can see Barak's unease. He would have been scared, as well as filled with anticipation of the battle. Perhaps he was seeking to call Deborah's bluff by saying, "You go up with me!" or perhaps his faith wasn't big enough to believe the Lord really would bring the victory.

Either way, Deborah's faith was certainly big enough. In response to his request, Deborah said, "I will go with you" (v. 9). As a woman who was strategic, Deborah needed to have an open mind, be perceptive and knowledgeable of what was happening around her, and be able to 'read' the landscape. She would have been proactive and looking to both make and take decisions based on the direction, wisdom and strength God had given her—much like Jael who made a shrewd plan to kill Sisera by driving a tent peg through his head. Of course, neither passage of scripture is encouraging us to attack our 'enemies' in this way to get rid of them. The revelation I get about Jael is that she was brave and bold as she carried out the strategy God had put in her heart. To be honest, if I was Jael, or even Deborah, I think I would have been saying to the Lord, "Please, is there another way that this can be done?"

Jeremiah 29:11 is a familiar verse that reassures us that God has purposes for our lives:

> *I know the plans I have for you, declares the Lord, plans to prosper you and not to harm you, plans to give you a future and a hope.*

God is a strategic planner! He has plans for us! From the beginning of time God has purposed and planned. In Genesis, and right through to Revelation, we see that God is outworking His plan to see His people restored. He doesn't wake up each morning and ask, "What will I get Maree to work on today?" No, He is the Alpha and the Omega. He knows the beginning from the end—He is the One who is and who was and who is come, the Almighty (Revelation 1:8). Does that not stir your spirit?!

Have you sought God regarding the strategic plans that He has for you? Have you written those plans down and put them into action? These strategic plans are not just going to drop into our lap—we need to sit with the Father and ask Him to open the scrolls of heaven and show us the projects, assignments and tasks we are to partner with Him on.

As a business strategist, a lot of this comes naturally to me. Strategic planning and thinking put a skip in my step. It is a strength I have been given, that ability to think about the future and put plans and actions in place. I acknowledge not all of us are this way inclined, and that it will be more challenging for some of us. However, I firmly believe that we all have the ability to be strategic, and it is something we must hone over time. Strategy is necessary if we are to turn plans into action steps.

When God first gave me the plan and action steps for the *Deborah Conference*, I thought the focus was just going to be the conference itself. However, as I have sat with the Lord over the years, He revealed to me more plans and action steps, one of which was to write this book. Another was to start up a series of *Deborah Women in Business* chapters in developing countries. The purpose of the *Deborah Women in Business Collective* is to strengthen, nurture, encourage and grow Christian women in self-sustaining business projects and opportunities. The heart for each chapter is to champion women to build microbusinesses that will generate income to support the needs of their family and sow into the needs of their community.

The first *Deborah Women in Business Collective* chapter was inaugurated in 2020 with the beautiful women of the Pentecostal Assembly of God in Katunda Village, Uganda, under the umbrella of the Barnabas Legacy Children's Dream Foundation. This chapter serves and impacts the Katunda community—and surrounding communities—through self-sustaining business projects, including projects which provide financial support and practical care for widows and orphans. Many times over, this chapter has caused my heart to burst with joy at what the Lord has done. God has added projects, and the women are achieving amazing outcomes. The current projects include tailoring, baking, farming crops such as maize and tomatoes, knitting and crocheting, mat-weaving and jewellery making. A group of women are taking part and learning the skills in each project. The chapter hired a small office and has since built a market stand outside where the farm produce is sold.

When we first started this chapter, the women did not know how to sew or bake or knit. With the support of some amazing donors, I purchased sewing machines, an electric and a charcoal oven, and hired a local tutor to teach tailoring and baking. It is incredible how fast the women have picked up these skills, and now, three years on, the women are looking forward to sewing the uniforms for the Agape Star Christian School. The baking has been a great fundraiser, and the farm harvest is amazing. Some of the maize and beans go to the school now, so that breakfast and lunch can be provided for the children.

The second *Deborah Women in Business Collective* chapter started in October 2021 with a small number of women who live in a leprosy colony in the Matigara district, Siliguri, in North-western India. I had the privilege of meeting people from this community when I was in Siliguri on a mission trip some years earlier. The Matigara chapter includes girls and women; some have leprosy themselves, while others are wives, daughters and mothers who care for those with leprosy. We now partner with another incredible God-breathed ministry called Shalom Nagar. This was founded by an amazing local pastor whose passion is to empower the community through sharing the love of Christ. She has a small team of volunteers who help guide the youth and children, buy medicine for the diseased, and support families by giving food and clothing. One of the long-term plans for this chapter is a small garden area where vegetables can be grown to help supply food and turn a profit by selling the surplus.

Cultivating a Strategic Spirit

One key principle I want our chapter leaders to understand is that as business owners, we need to be strategic. We cannot be all things to all people, otherwise we will run ourselves ragged and end up with a business barely breaking even. In that case, we might as well go back to a conventional employment role. If that sounds like you, here are four simple and practical questions to kick-start some strong strategic decision-making for your business:

1. **What challenges are you solving for your customers or the clients you serve?**

For example, you might be a career counsellor and one of the challenges you solve is helping your clients transition from their previous role into a new role in a new industry. Once you have a clearer idea of what the challenges are for your customers and clients, you can start to address them through the products and services you offer.

2. **What is your business' unique value proposition (UVP), also known as your 'unique selling point'?**

A value proposition outlines what your business will do for your customers and clients that will drive your business success and provide relief from their problems. There is no one-size-fits-all template when writing a UVP, but it helps to start by thinking about the pain points of your target market. For example, if you sell a skincare range for those who struggle with oily skin, you UVP might be something like: "Oily skin problems no more! Our products are guaranteed to take away that unwanted shine, once and for all!"

3. What is the current reality in your business?

Reflect on the challenges your customers or clients have, and on the UVP for your business. Next, look at what you are doing across an average week in your business. Is what you are doing—your tasks, actions, phone calls, administration—aligned to solving your customers' challenges and delivering on your USP? Maybe you are spending too much time on Facebook posts when your target market are not big Facebook users? Or your prices may be too low, so you have to squeeze too many clients in each week, leaving you tired and unable to give your best? Whatever it is, take a reality check!

4. What obstacles and barriers do you face? What can you do to navigate through those?

Having identified your current reality, it is time to look at the obstacles and barriers. You might have to deal with some hard truths! Are you posting on social media because you like to be in control and the thought of someone else doing the marketing just doesn't seem right, yet it is eating up five hours of potential client time a week? Knowing the underlying reasons you are doing something will help you to come up with solutions that enable you to overcome the obstacles and barriers. This will leave you better able to serve your clients, align with your UVP, and have greater business success.

You can apply the same questions to your personal and ministry life as well. If you run a youth group ministry for example, what challenges are you solving for the young people in your group? What is at the heart of the ministry—the 'uniqueness' of what you are doing? Is this just another youth group for the sake of it, or has God shown you the uniqueness of this youth group? Perhaps the strategic emphasis is on imparting His unconditional love to the attendees. Define your UVP! Then ask, what is the current reality in the youth ministry? What are the main barriers and obstacles? What can you change in order to better serve the young people and align to the mandate, the 'uniqueness' that God has shown you for this youth ministry?

I want to assure you that strategy leads to 'spoils', or in other words, successful results. If you are strategic in partnering with God, and outwork the plans He has shown you, then you will have success; it will be well with you. Read the account of Sisera's mother in Judges 5. There we see a woman who presumed her son would win the battle and was impatiently waiting, not only for his return, but for all the spoils of war he would bring home with him:

> *Through the window peered Sisera's mother; behind the lattice, she cried out, 'Why is his chariot so long in coming? Why is the clatter of his chariots delayed?' The wisest of her ladies answer her; indeed, she keeps saying to herself, 'Are they not finding and dividing the spoils: a woman or two for each man, colourful garments as plunder for Sisera, colourful garments embroidered, highly embroidered garments for my neck—all this as plunder?'*
> — *Judges 5:28-30*

But there were no spoils coming home that day, because Sisera's army had lost the battle and he was, in fact, dead. Barak and his army had won! They had, in the strength of their God, routed the enemy. It was Barak and the people of God who were gathering the spoils.

God is the victor. He has the final say, not the enemy who comes to steal, kill and destroy (John 10:10). It is time to arise and go forth like King David, to take back that which the enemy has stolen; it is time to bring home the spoils.

> *So David recovered all that the Amalekites had carried away, and David rescued his two wives. And nothing of theirs was lacking, either small or great, sons or daughters, spoil or anything which they had taken from them; David recovered all.*
> — 1 Samuel 30:18-19 NKJV

I take great comfort in the fact that God is a restorer. He will "restore the years the locusts have eaten" (Joel 2:25). I sometimes think about my challenging childhood years and how those years have impacted me as an adult. I have this sense that I have lost years—years when I could have felt more secure, loved, fulfilled and happy, instead of sad and alone. But I chose to put a line in the sand, and to say to the enemy (as the Lord did regarding Job), "Thus far and no further" (Job 38:11). It's time for recompense—for the spoils of battle to be returned. I love the verse:

> *Come back to the place of safety, all you prisoners who still have hope! I promise this very day that I will repay two blessings for each of your troubles.*
> — Zechariah 9:12 NLT

In other words, God will give us double for our trouble! Isaiah 61:7 says, "Instead of your shame you will receive a double portion, and instead of disgrace you will rejoice in your inheritance. And so you will inherit a double portion in your land, and everlasting joy will be yours." A double portion is mine, and it is yours!

Reflection Questions

1. On a scale of one to five (five being the highest), how would you rate yourself in terms of being strategic? Are there areas of your life where you feel you are more strategic than in others? For example, would you rate yourself quite highly when it comes to being strategic in business, but for your personal wellbeing and health you would rate yourself lower?

2. Consider the keys to cultivating a strategic way of operating in your life. Go through each recommendation and journal your responses. Do this for your business and ministry life. Pray over what God shows you and what changes and actions you need to take.

3. In your personal life, is there an area where there has been a lot of loss, an area in which you feel bereaved? Take this to the Lord and sit with Him awhile. Ask Him to bring His healing presence into this area of your life in a greater way. Linger until you feel reassured in the knowledge that He is a God who restores and that in Him nothing is lost or wasted.

CHAPTER EIGHT

She is Purposeful

I FLATTED WITH SEVERAL other students during my time at university in Wellington. One night as I was washing, stacking and putting away dishes, one of my flatmates called out to me as she passed by the kitchen, "Maree, is there anything you do that doesn't have a purpose? You even do the dishes purposefully!" For some reason this incident has always stayed with me. At first, I felt a bit hurt by what she said, as I thought she was mocking me. However, when I asked her why she'd made the comment, she replied: "There is just this way about you. Even the smallest tasks, you do them with the end goal in mind."

Being purposeful means to have determination and show resolve, to have a sense of purpose. I have always found that being purposeful comes naturally to me. The opposite spirit, I suppose, would be aimlessness, thoughtlessness, a lack of determination and planning. The children of Israel wandered in the wilderness for forty years because they were not purposeful. They became aimless, lost their direction and drive, and forgot that the wilderness wasn't intended to be a destination. They were to pass *through* the wilderness, not stay *in* it. I don't want to find myself in that situation.

While I believe all we do—dishes included—should be done to the glory of God, I also know that, for good mental wellbeing, we need pockets of time where we are aimless, carefree and unplanned. Over the years I have had to learn how to be more spontaneous and go with the flow—travelling with my husband has done that for me! We can be on holiday driving between Point A and Point B, but Mr Adventurer (as I have nicknamed him) will have us go to Points X, L and S before we even reach Point B. He is someone who really enjoys the journey, whereas I am a 'let's get to the destination right now!' kind of person.

Like a lot of things in life, it's about balance. We are not robots. God created us for frivolity, silliness, and times of spontaneity as much as He has created us for purpose and resolve. Even Deborah, no doubt, took moments of 'off-duty' time to relax and recharge. These pockets of time are vital if we are to be at our best and, when our moment comes, we will be ready to step up and step out in faith.

> *Villagers in Israel would not fight; they held back until I, Deborah, arose . . .*
>
> *— Judges 5:7(emphasis mine)*

This is a verse I go back to time and time again. Because Deborah arose to that which God had put in her heart and hands to do, the enemy was routed and the children of Israel were freed from King Jabin's reign of terror. Deborah was purposeful, and as a result, the course of history was shifted! There are many biblical examples of men and women who changed the course of history because they stepped up, determined and resolute in their God. Think of Joshua, Nehemiah, Esther, Paul . . . they all participated in seeing His Kingdom come.

SHE IS PURPOSEFUL

In Judges chapter 4 we see that Deborah was not only purposeful as a judge (v. 5), strongly and powerfully passing down judgements, laying out the law, and calling to Barak to gather the army and go to battle. She was also purposeful as a leader (v. 6), encourager (v. 9), visionary and prophet (v. 14). No wonder Deborah needed to be firm in her purpose! I don't think Israel would have necessarily responded to her prophetic words with a round of applause or cries of, "Sure Deborah, we will get on to that straight away!" Perhaps she was mocked. Perhaps people said things like, "Who do you think you are, telling us what to do and where to go and what the Lord is saying?" But Deborah knew her God-given role and was confident in hearing the voice of God. As a result, she was able to stand firm in her purpose.

Naturally speaking, we prefer ease and comfort. Yet we are only on this earth for a short time. We are not here merely to skip through the fields and smell the tulips, to be aimless wanderers. God has given us 'land' to possess! We must awake (get up), arise (get going), and take new ground in the market or sphere God has appointed for us.

It has been my personal experience that there may be some dis-ease and discomfort as we awake and arise. There are times when you may be misunderstood or even scoffed at. But the greatest antidote to this is to simply go out and do what the Lord has told you! Sometimes I have kept what God has whispered to me hidden in my heart because in sharing it, I have received incredulous reactions and comments like, "How do you think you will manage that?" or, "Isn't your life already busy enough?" However, you know what? Actions speak louder than words. My choice, like Deborah's, is to look to the Helper. Our help comes from the Lord who created heaven and earth (Psalm 121:1), the strength of our life (Psalm 27:1).

A few years ago, God gave me a vision in which I saw the most incredible library. I am a lover of books, so as you can imagine, I walked around the shelves with great delight, excitement, and awe. On one of the shelves were sets of books with my name down the spine (I couldn't stop thinking, wow!), while other shelves held sets of books authored by friends and acquaintances. I was struck by the fact they were *sets of books*—not just a book, or books.

I opened some of the books and was amazed at what fell out: a cascade of musical notes; an amazing collection of words that danced before my eyes; big, bold statements that I saw were going to impact governments, policy and legislation; words of healing, breakthrough, authority, innovation, solutions, directions, plans. Words, words . . . and more words.

Later I reflected in my journal: *God needs His writers to write!* God has much He wants to download to His people in this hour. I believe God has songs, poems, speeches, policy, books (fiction and non-fiction), blogs, social media posts, equations, guides, devotionals, journals, manuals, research papers, scripts for plays, films, documentaries and so on. I felt the urgency in my spirit as God reiterated, "Maree, my writers need to write."

As I took this vision to prayer, I felt God encourage me to begin writing a couple of books—one on lessons from the life of Deborah, and the other on taking the leap from employment into self-employment as a mid-life professional woman. I had previously written some e-books, but never a chapter book. I had also helped others with their books—the structure, how to shape their stories and so on, but had not done this for myself. How hard could it be, right? I had the experience and the skill, and most importantly, I had our faithful God!

But then life happened—you know, the ins and outs, the ups and downs, the distractions, the discouragement, the Covid-19 pandemic. And in the midst of it all, God spoke to me again about writing books. He reminded me that I needed to be purposeful—determined, resourceful, and intentional, so I set out a plan, got a book writing mentor, and joined a book writing membership. I opened a Google document and gave it a title—Draft One. I scheduled 'writing appointments' into my calendar, and little by little, words emerged. I had begun!

And then I got struck by covid. For months, the covid cough and fatigue chased my tail—so much so that I felt I was going down a sinking hole. I had promised myself that my two books would be at the publisher before my fifty-sixth birthday, but this did not happen. I had fallen off the wagon in terms of being purposeful. But the reality is that life and sickness do get in the way. We *are* human after all, and sometimes I think we forget that!

Thankfully, I began to emerge from this difficult season. In prayer, the Lord gave me Ecclesiastes 10:10: "If the axe is dull and he does not sharpen its edge, then he must exert more strength; but wisdom [to sharpen the axe] helps him succeed [with less effort]" (AMP). I knew when I read those words that my 'axe head' of writing had become dull; I had not kept it sharp—I had dropped the ball. *Ouch.* I knew it . . . but it hurt to say it aloud. Lots of tears and time with God later, I emerged with renewed purpose to write as He had told me to do. I set out my plan again, scheduled time in my calendar, re-engaged with my writing mentor and writing club, got the book cover designed, and put up a promotion about it. I knew that the Lord would help me cross the finish line. As I put my shoulder to the plough, He has enabled me and guided my work.

Cultivating a Purposeful Life

We all go through periods of being stalled. Do you often find yourself feeling very aimless and wandering around? Here are some ways to cultivate a purposeful life:

Lean into Your Identity in Christ

Knowing you are a child of God and leaning into your identity (rather than letting it merely be words) is central to walking out the purposes and plans God has for you. You are so loved by the Father! He rejoices over you with singing (Zephaniah 3:17). He surrounds you with songs of deliverance (Psalm 32:7). His banner over you is love (Song of Solomon 2:4). Picture a child who is nurtured and championed by their parents. A child with that kind of love and support lives differently from a child without it. They are confident, willing to try new things. They can set about their day with clarity about who they are, regardless of what they have to do.

Not all of us have experienced this as children. Perhaps, like me, you have had to battle with low self-esteem and poor confidence and at times you find yourself questioning your identity in God—*if your parents rejected you, then surely God does too?* That is a lie from the pit of hell. Our God never rejects us! Keep leaning into the Father, asking Him to strengthen your knowledge and assurance that you are His. It is in knowing that you belong to Him and are loved by Him that you can go about your life with purpose, resolve and determination.

Understand and Use Your Skills and Talents

Get to know, understand and increase your awareness of what makes you tick. What are your gifts, and how are you using them? This is a question some people find difficult. They are either unsure and say, "I don't really have any skills or talents," or they are hesitant to share them out loud, fearing it might sound like showing off. Yes, God has called us to be humble, but He has not called us to hide our talents. Imagine if Deborah refused to use her legal or conflict resolution skills or held back in her ability to declare and prophecy what God was saying. How different would Israel's history have been?

If this is an area you struggle with, start by seeking out books or people to help you unpack your skills and talents. All of us have natural gifting just waiting to be uncovered and put to work! Think of the parable of the talents in Matthew 25:14-30. To one servant, the master gave one talent; to another, five; and, to another, ten. This parable is not about how many skills and gifts you have been given. The point is that we are to use what God has given us to the best of our ability, and if we do that, God rewards us with still more talents to use for His Kingdom.

Do What Puts a Spring in Your Step

Think about what makes you feel alive and energetic, then get out and do it! Doing something is better than doing nothing! It is action that activates. What gets you out of bed on a frosty morning? No, you do not have to answer with a super-spiritual response. Is it the thought of going to your local café and having a delicious coffee because you love the warmth and buzz of people, and a hot drink helps you 'arise' for the day? This would be my husband—he is such a lover of people, and the early morning café vibe is invigorating to him. Meanwhile, his wife just wants to get into her office, open the laptop, and spend a power hour doing her writing!

It is in the simple, ordinary matters of our day that we become aware of what moves our heart and what puts a skip in our steps. It is that movement and those steps that underlie our sense of purpose.

Create an Action Plan

However much you lean into your identity in God, understand and explore your skills, or are aware of what moves your heart, if no action comes as a result, then all you have done is *awaken*; you have not *arisen*.

To arise is to take action. You can wake in the morning, open your eyes, and stretch your arms, but it is not until you put your feet on the ground and move that you begin to rise. That's why it's helpful to have an action plan. You don't need an action plan for every area of your life, but you can use a diary or an app to help you purposefully track towards your goals. For example, if you want to grow in God's Word, you might put in your action plan to attend a bible study group and one night a week to do your bible study at home. If God has showed you a new income stream to add to your business, *What do you need to do? How are you going to do it? Whose help do you need? What timeframes will you work to? What due dates will you set for the actions you have proposed?*

Mighty Deborahs arise through action!

LORD, I WILL WRITE

Books, and books, and more books.
In every corner, in every nook.
Chapter upon chapter, line upon line.
Oh, I just want to look and look.
My fingers run along the spines.

As my eyes dash across the many titles,

My heart is jumping with delight.

So much to see, oh what a sight.

I see my name upon a book.

I look, oh my, my name is upon books!

"Lord, what are these volumes?" I ask.

He smiles and whispers: "This is your task."

In my hand, He places a pen. It is made of fine gold.

Oh my, but it is so heavy to hold.

"Take it," He says, "Now take this pen,

Now go, write, and write.

Indeed, just continue to write,

For I need My writers to write."

As we mature in the Lord, we come to understand that yes, He is gracious, yes, He is patient and longsuffering towards us—that is His nature and character. But as co-heirs, we too must do our part, otherwise our tasks may be put in the hands of another. I do not want to be found not to have fulfilled the history-making assignments, projects and ventures that He has given me, and I am sure you do not want that either.

I do want you to know, however, that there is no condemnation to those who are in Christ (Romans 8:1). The human experience is one that Jesus has been through. One of the impacts of my childhood challenges and some very tough seasons is that I have battled with depression and anxiety and have been diagnosed with complex post-traumatic stress disorder. This is not easy to put down on paper. It takes a lot of vulnerability for me to write it, but I have chosen to live both the good stuff and the hard stuff 'out loud' for the glory of God.

I want to encourage you that while God calls us, urges us, and convicts us to be about our Father's business, He is also our Abba Father. Romans 8:14-16 says:

> *For those who are led by the Spirit of God are the children of God. The Spirit you received does not make you slaves, so that you live in fear again; rather, the Spirit you received brought about your adoption to sonship. f And by him we cry, "Abba, g Father." The Spirit himself testifies with our spirit that we are God's children.*

God has unconditional love and compassion for us. On some days, to get myself out of bed, do a load of washing, and work in my business for a couple of hours is all I can manage. Sometimes I can feel very low and sad, and I can't shake it. In these seasons, I keep pressing in for God's healing, I seek help, I put strategies in place to help me regulate my emotions better, I choose to avoid certain situations and people if they are triggers, and I choose not to guilt-trip myself. I am leaning into God's promises for my life, knowing they are "yes and amen" (2 Corinthians 1:20). In His hands my adversity and sorrows can be turned into service for the glory, honour and praise of His name.

Whatever personal pain, sorrow and challenges you navigate life with—dear reader, your God has your back, now and always!

Reflection Questions

1. Is there a project, assignment or vision God dropped into your heart some time ago, but due to whatever reasons, you feel like your 'axe head' has become dull? Pull out your journal and write some action steps you could do to get yourself going again—to *arise*. Commit those action steps to the Lord, asking for His help. Remember He can do exceedingly abundantly more than what we ask or think (Ephesians 3:20)!

2. Is there a faith hero in your life, someone you would describe as extremely intentional, determined and resourceful in what they do? Make a coffee date (offline or online) with them. Share your experience, then ask for any key tips or advice they may have for keeping focussed on what the Lord has assigned them to do.

3. Identify the men and women in the Bible who inspire you to be purposeful. I personally read the book of Nehemiah on repeat! Nehemiah set about the task God had given him—to rebuild the broken walls of Jerusalem—and it was completed in fifty-two days! (Nehemiah 6:15). Take time to study the purposeful men and women of the Bible. Be ready to glean from their lives and apply what you learn to your own life.

CHAPTER NINE

SHE IS ENCOURAGING

Being a spiritual encourager requires seeing the one you are speaking over through the Father's eyes, as one He created and knitted together (Psalm 139) for God's Kingdom purposes. Deborah was masterful at this. Throughout Judges 4 and 5, we see her encouraging Barak to rise up into the calling God placed on his life. It was she who encouraged Barak to gather the army and face the enemy.

Words of encouragement are powerful. They are an opportunity to declare life over the listener—reminding them of the strengths that are in them and the dreams, hopes and aspirations that may have become buried by their life journey. The encourager is the one who pours strength and hope into the listener.

We all need to feel loved and confident in ourselves, and to have people around us who motivate us in our mission is invaluable. When I was a child, I never received much encouragement, perhaps a little, but usually words were used to highlight what I couldn't do, or to state that I wouldn't amount to anything. I developed very poor self-esteem and low confidence, and it has taken me years to form a healthier opinion of myself. Despite this experience as a child, one thing I determined early in my adult years was that I would be an encourager. Encouragement can be like a refreshing brook on a very hot day; whether it's a smile, a few kind words, a card of encouragement or prayer for a person, it truly is, to paraphrase Acts 20:35, more blessed to give encouragement than it is even to receive it.

Something I love about Deborah was that she stayed beside Barak all the way; partnering with him in battle and encouraging him to run in his God-given assignment. Think for a moment what would have happened if Deborah had allowed herself to be intimidated by Jabin's army and not accompanied Barak into battle —the enemy would not have been defeated, the children of Israel would have remained in chaos and dysfunction, and Barak would have felt a complete and utter failure. Isn't it sobering when you think about this? No victory would have happened apart from Deborah, who stepped into this window of history and took action to encourage another. Wow, that is the type of person I want to be! I want my words and actions to encourage another to the extent that the world is changed by it.

You know what it feels like when you want to pursue something new—it might be a new type of job you haven't done before, or a business idea you want to try, or some health changes you want to make. When you don't receive feedback or encouragement, what happens? Most likely, you find it hard to stick to any goals you have set, and you want to quit. You can end up feeling discouraged and despondent, wondering why you ever wanted to start on that new thing anyway.

One thing I want us to particularly take note of is that encouragement does not necessarily mean that our words are 'all sunshine and roses'. Encouragement needs to be truthful, not puffed-up, fancy words designed only to lift a person's ego. Encouragement requires words and actions that go right to the heart and soul. Deborah encouraged Barak to gather his army and go up to battle, but in that encouragement she also told Barak that the final victory would come through the hands of a woman and not through him.

Then, at the end of Judges chapter four we read how Barak went out to meet Jael, and she showed him Sisera, the commander of the Canaanite army, whom she had killed:

> *Just then Barak came by in pursuit of Sisera, and Jael went out to meet him. "Come," she said, "I will show you the man you're looking for." So he went in with her, and there lay Sisera with the tent peg through his temple—dead.*
> — *Judges 4:22*

Again, I want us to pause and think about Barak's reaction to Deborah earlier on. He could have said, "Excuse me? Victory through a woman? That won't be happening! I will have the victory, not another!" But because Deborah's encouragement had been spoken with wisdom, love, deep compassion, and an understanding of that hour in history, Barak received it without taking offence. What Deborah prophesied came to pass. The victory, the defeat of the commander, came through a woman.

∼

The Word of God not only encourages us personally but also shows us the importance of championing and supporting those around us—it urges us to spur others on, to build people up. Can you imagine the impact on your community, neighbours, business, and schools if there was more encouragement; if we cheered on our workmates, our business associates, our church leadership? What a change we would see! Think of some scriptures to meditate on regarding the power of encouragement. For example, Hebrews 10:24-25 urges us to "consider how we may spur one another on toward love and good deeds, not giving up meeting together, as some are in the habit of doing, but encouraging one another—and all the more as you see the Day approaching." Romans 15:2 tells us, "Each of us should please our neighbours for their good, to build them up." 1 Thessalonians 5:11 shares the sentiment: "Therefore encourage one another and build each other up, just as in fact you are doing."

I love encouraging young people to pursue their education and thrive in their gifts and talents—this is one of the reasons I took such delight in co-founding a school. I can't wait until we add a secondary campus on to our kindergarten and primary set-up in a couple of years' time. Across my fifteen-year teaching career I was always in trouble with the principal for doing things outside the box! Once a principal found me with my boys' maths class out on the rugby field where I was teaching them their times tables using a fitness routine and a rugby ball!

I loved it when I got the opportunity to be a principal of a new school for its founding years; I sought to be innovative and to make learning fun, practical, impactful and life-building for the students. Whether it was camps or coaching water polo, I was there! Half the time, I didn't know what I was doing, but I sure was the students' biggest cheerleader. My first school camp (literally!) was a fishing camp. The students thought it was hilarious that I had never fished before—let alone put up a tent or cooked baked beans on a camp gas cooker! But as I stood on the banks of the lake learning how to fly-fish, my heart was happy to be there. I decided to bolster the students by offering a prize for the first fish caught. Obviously, I knew it was not going to be me, and I wanted some fish for the evening meal, so this seemed a good way to ensure I got some food. I love God's sense of humour! Guess who caught the very first fish of the camp? Yes, me! You see, being an encourager has its rewards! By the way, I still gave the prize to the first student who caught a fish.

I count it a privilege to have had the opportunity to pour into those students. They brought youthful exuberance, laughter, noise, silliness, and certainly no pockets of silence. Those teaching years fed and restored my soul after having grown up in a silent household. In my last teaching gig, which was in Adelaide, the students gave me the 'Megaphone Award' at the end-of-year awards event. At first, I was aghast that they would choose that—surely, I was not *that* loud (remember quiet, shy me?). They said I was being given this award because if they needed to see me for something or wanted encouragement or support with their work, they would stand outside in the courtyard and listen for my laughter. When they heard the laughter, they knew where to find me! Truly our God is so good; from being a 'silent' person to being known for my not-so-silent (indeed, loud!) laugh which was a signal of encouragement to these young people; that right there shows our miracle working God!

As a teacher I always gravitated towards the children who were broken, crushed, painfully shy, vulnerable to bullies, unloved, and seemingly unwanted by parents. As I worked among the students my heart was moved time and time again, and that was when God began to whisper to me about retraining in law, specialising in child protection. I started my law degree part-time. I clearly remember on Day One, as they put up photos of men and women with incredible legal minds, I felt a prayer rising in my spirit: "Lord, may I be a voice for the voiceless." I felt a stirring to encourage the broken and bruised to come awake and to arise in the healing, unconditional love of the Father. This rising from within has flowed through every business and ministry venture and community project that I have been, and am, involved in.

I once had a lovely, quiet woman with some challenging health issues come and speak with me about wanting to start a photography business. I asked her if she had some photos she could show me. She replied no, she hadn't taken any photos. Oh, I thought to myself, feeling a bit perplexed. I continued talking with her, asking what sort of camera she liked to use when taking photos. She replied, "I do not have a camera." Oh, I thought again. I asked what type of photos she would like to work on, and suddenly she came to life. She said she would like to take photos of nature, of waterways, trees and flowers, and then maybe put a scripture on the photos and sell them as an encouragement gift card or postcard. Right, I had a starting point! My head and heart went into action!

We went off to the camera store and she picked out a camera and put it on layby for a few weeks until she would have it paid off. Then she started to practise taking photos. She didn't have a car, so I took her out to a few spots. At first, the photos had a lot of blurring and an array of interesting angles! Through a contact, I was able to get her some photography coaching sessions. Once she had a few quality photos, I sourced her a refurbished laptop for her fledgling business and showed her how to use Canva to put a scripture onto a photo. Together we developed a logo, tagline, and decided on the branding colours for her business.

A few months later, this amazing woman started to sell her photos, and she got great sales! Today she sells a range of products with her prints on them and has even had a couple of photo books produced. That is the power of encouragement! It's step by step! This woman is radiant, confident, happy, and shares the love of God and her business with every person she meets. I can see such a change in her compared to when I met her four years ago.

CULTIVATING A SPIRIT OF ENCOURAGEMENT

It is all very well for us to say, "I want to be an encourager," but how does one truly go about that? Here are some small steps that I have found useful in my own life.

Hone in on Strengths

Encouragement needs to flow freely and be authentic. We must be real and honest with our praise. If encouragement is not your strong suit, you might find it a bit awkward at first. Focus on what someone has done right instead of what they do wrong. If you are a manager in a workplace, this can sometimes be hard to do, particularly when you are under stress and there are outcomes to meet and your team members are not doing their part. In situations such as these, my motto is: "work their strengths". Find the strengths that person has, and hone in on them, delegating tasks that enable their superpower to shine. Remember, the moon was not created for the daytime, and the sun was not created for the night. It's the same with people!

Applaud Small Steps

One thing my mum always repeated was the saying, "Rome was not built in a day." For some reason those words always irked me. As I got older, I found myself fighting to try and build Rome yesterday rather than today! In other words, though well intentioned, I would sometimes get too far ahead of myself, and of God, and I had to remind myself that the tortoise and the hare both finished the race. Sometimes I could sense God's smile as He looked down and gently berated me saying, "Maree, I am back here! Why are you trying to go so far ahead? That is only going to lead you into worrying and fretting." Surprise, surprise, God was right!

I say all this to show that I have had to work hard at encouraging people's small efforts—efforts which may appear little, but to the person who has done them, having their effort applauded can mean so much. In fact, recognising one little step can encourage the person to continue with more and more steps. It is a way of helping a small effort grow into something large. As we read in Zechariah 4:10, "Do not despise these small beginnings, for the Lord rejoices to see the work begin" (NLT).

Demonstrate Encouragement

Deborah's encouragement to Barak was demonstrated by her willingness to go up to battle with him. My way of encouraging my students to fish was to offer a prize! My way to encourage my business coaching client to start her photography business was to take her to the camera shop. Our encouragement needs to be demonstrated—both in our words and in our actions. You know how much children love to receive a star or happy face on their work, or to be awarded badges and certificates. We all have that small child inside of us. When I was a principal, I loved to think of ways to not only encourage the students, but also my staff. Sometimes it might be something as simple as some chocolates in their workbox or throwing an end-of-term luncheon to thank them for their efforts. As business owners, what can we do to encourage others in business? Maybe it's simply liking and sharing their social media posts. In any case, let's be women who actively demonstrate our encouragement!

Say Something Positive

As you pass people at work, at school or while out shopping, where appropriate, pause to say something positive about them: "I love the colour of your shirt"; "Saw your big kid at the skatepark last week and they were so kind to a little fella who took a fall"; "So lovely to have you in the neighbourhood"... and so on. People love to hear how others perceive them, because a lot of us are our own worst critic. Try and give concrete examples when you say something great about a person, so they can clearly see you are not just saying those words for flattery. To point out to someone how kind, caring, thoughtful, timely or innovative they are, is life-giving.

Be Upbeat

Be someone who others like to be around! Your smile, your laughter, your caring nature and desire to be present with people, will draw them to you and provide encouragement. *Are you the one who opens a door for a person, or lets someone with a small amount of shopping go before you at the supermarket counter? Do you give a small, pleasant wave when your neighbour takes their driveway too fast and knocks over your rubbish bin by accident... for the third time?* Life is challenging, and you never know what situation a person may be facing. I am not saying that we must be a Pollyanna twenty-four seven, but we need to be mindful that God has called us to encourage others and to keep a check on ourselves. Are our words, actions, attitudes, and outlook on life praiseworthy? The Bible says, "Finally, brethren, whatever things are true, whatever things are noble, whatever things are just, whatever things are pure, whatever things are lovely, whatever things are of good report, if there is any virtue and if there is anything praiseworthy—meditate on these things" (Philippians 4:8, NKJV).

> *For many will come in my name, claiming, 'I am the Messiah,' and will deceive many. You will hear of wars and rumours of wars, but see to it that you are not alarmed. Such things must happen, but the end is still to come. Nation will rise against nation, and kingdom against kingdom. There will be famines and earthquakes in various places. All these are the beginning of birth pains. (Matthew 24:5-8).*

If ever the world needs encouragers to speak up, it is now. Day by day, we are moving closer to our Lord's return. It is easy to become overwhelmed. In the past year, the world has faced war in Ukraine, earthquakes in Turkey and Syria, flooding and cyclones in New Zealand, severe famine in central Yemen . . . the list could go on and on.

We only need to watch the news each day to be bombarded with 'bad news'. It can be so discouraging, and as a result, many are without hope, despondent and fearful. Since the arrival of Covid-19, I have noticed people are more highly strung, seemingly waiting for the next disaster to occur. Parents are afraid of what the world will be like for their children, business owners are anxious about whether there is going to be a financial crash . . . the possibilities seem increasingly gloomy.

Mighty Deborah, you have the antidote! Will you step forward at this critical point of history—as Deborah did in her time—and encourage people with the good news of the gospel of Jesus Christ? The power of what He has done on the cross—taking our sins, our diseases, our worries, our burdens upon Himself—cannot be understated. The most powerful encouragement you can give to those who are in and around your life in this hour is your knowledge of the Saviour. Tell them your testimonies of what the Lord has done for you. Revelation 12:11 says, "And they overcame him by the blood of the Lamb, and by the word of their testimony" (NKJV). Likewise, 1 Peter 3:15 urges us to, "always be ready to give a [logical] defence to anyone who asks you to account for the hope and confident assurance [elicited by faith] that is within you, yet [do it] with gentleness and respect" (AMP).

Reflection Questions

1. Who has God called you to encourage, champion, lift and build up in order to see them through to a place of victory? Write these names down in your journal, then pray and speak over their lives, seeking the Lord for a scripture to intercede for them.

2. Who might be on the edges in your life that seems unlikely (in the eyes of man) to be able to do anything in God because there is always something troubling or distressing them or they try things and fail? What can you do to help them fly again?

3. Decide each day to send an encouraging text to a friend, family member or work colleague. I do this regularly, though not necessarily daily. It is a great habit to have; the power of encouraging others can be life changing—for them and for you.

4. Reflect on who you have shared the gospel with lately. Who have you shared your testimonies—the stories of what the Lord has done in your life—with? Ask the Lord to give you opportunities to share with others the hope and confidence you have in Him.

CHAPTER TEN

SHE IS ACTION-ORIENTED

As I reflect on what we read about Deborah in the book of Judges, I see that she held prayer and praise in one hand, and purpose and action in the other. God calls us both to be and to do—to *be with Him* and then *do with Him*. We are His hands and feet in a broken and dying world that needs to know the grace and mercy of a Saviour who gave His life for us, taking our pain and burdens upon the cross. In Judges chapter five we read of those who *did not* take action when the Lord commanded the people to awaken and to arise:

> *In the districts of Reuben, there was much searching of heart. Why did you stay among the sheep pens to hear the whistling for the flocks? . . . Gilead stayed beyond the Jordan. And Dan, why did he linger by the ships? Asher remained on the coast and stayed in his coves.*
> — *Judges 5:15-17*

The princes of Issachar took action, but those of the tribe of Reuben fled to the back fields, away from the impending battle. The tribe of Gilead likewise stayed beyond the Jordan; there was no way they wanted to get involved! As for the tribe of Dan, they just loitered by their ships, not wanting to leave their comfort zone, not wanting to do something different, something riskier than what they already knew. Wow, that is a hard-hitting criticism! I know I am often guilty of wanting to remain in my own comfort zone. Are you also?

But it is the tribe of Asher that concerns me most. They stayed up the coast, away from where the battle was about to take place. Not only that, but they hid themselves away. The tribe of Asher wanted to make certain no one was going to come and ask for their help. How often are we like that, shying away from the 'battles' and keeping our head down when there is a need for people to take action? It's easy to hide in our caves of mediocrity, to keep silent and tuck ourselves away. There needs to be much searching of the heart when our inaction is holding us back from our Lord's call to awaken, His call to arise. The tribes of Issachar, Reuben, Dan and Ephraim, and the city of Meroz paid a hefty prince for their reluctance to help the people of God. We read:

> *"Curse Meroz," said the angel of the LORD. "Curse its people bitterly, because they did not come to help the LORD, to help the LORD against the mighty."*
>
> — *Judges 5:22-23*

Where will you be found when the heat and discomfort are turned up? Would you rather be found in the waters of discomfort, allowing the Father to shape you and mould you for His Kingdom purposes, or would you rather be on safe, calm seas where everything is steady, safe and storm-free? My own walk with God has shown me that it is the discomfort of the stormy seas, far from a safe harbour and where the promised land can only be seen as a speck in the distance that you find God like never before. There, you will find Him in a deep and abiding way. You will learn there that He is the God who will not fail you, nor forsake you, that He has not forgotten you or tossed you aside. Psalm 23 says that even when we walk through the valley of the shadow of death (or discomfort, dis-ease, disease, pain, misunderstanding, injustice, or whatever it is that we may be facing), we will fear no evil, for God's rod—His Word, and His staff—His Holy Spirit, will comfort us.

Let's look now at the tribes that *did* take action, Zebulun and Naphtali. They risked their lives, for in their God they knew there was no other option. They were ready to awake, arise, and go to battle.

> *The people of Zebulun risked their very lives; so did Naphtali on the terraced fields. "Kings came, they fought, the kings of Canaan fought. . . From the heavens the stars fought, from their courses, they fought against Sisera. The river Kishon swept them away, the age-old river, the river Kishon. March on, my soul; be strong!*
> — Judges 5:18-21

Oh how those words stir and encourage my heart! I do not want to be found sleeping or in a place of inaction when my God has called me to rise and take hold of the land that I am to possess. These two tribes rose to fight because they knew the One who would be in the heat of the battle with them. Even creation was on their side as they went to fight!

As modern-day Deborahs we are called to march on in our God and to command our souls to be strong! We might feel weak, we might feel inadequate, we might feel under-skilled, but when we are weak, our God is strong (2 Corinthians 12:8-9)! Strength to face a battle is not found in our human effort; it is found only as we nestle into the Father's heart, as we tune our ear to His songs of deliverance (Psalm 32:7). We must get to the point of being unafraid to take action when God calls us to do so—we are to be strong and of good courage, because He is the Lord our God who is with us (Joshua 1:9). Let's be action-orientated, like the tribes of Zebulun, Naphtali, Benjamin, Issachar and Makir—a city named for the son of Manasseh—and saddle up, galloping forth to take possession of the land that God has placed before us.

By nature, I am an action-orientated person. However, I have found that as I have gotten older, I have become, at times, more hesitant to act upon what God has spoken to me. Reflecting on why this has happened, I realise I have allowed fear and anxiety to intimidate me at times. When life has given you knocks, there is a vulnerability that sits in your heart. This can cause your emotions to be all over the place. Add in peri- and post-menopausal hormones, and that sense of vulnerability only builds. If I allow them to, fear and anxiety can become my Achilles' heel, holding me back.

I know some of you may also resonate with this. Thankfully, I know the cure. We need to seek God and work through those fears and anxieties while sitting at His feet. We need to identify our fears and spend time with the Father to allow Him to impart, heal and bring breakthrough. The enemy wants to smash our dreams and cause us to be inactive. The enemy has come to rob, steal and destroy, but we serve and walk with the King of kings and the Lord of lords. He is the victor, and through Him we have victory.

In my early fifties, God opened up an opportunity for my hubby and I to be able to purchase our own home in rural Australia. It was a friend who seeded this idea in my mind. My initial thought was, *but how?* We were getting on in years. What bank would look at us favourably for a mortgage? Secondly, we didn't quite have enough for a deposit. Despite those doubts, however, we decide to take some action steps. We began looking at houses. We decided what we liked and didn't like, spoke to a mortgage broker, contacted a real estate agent, had an appointment with the bank, and did some number-crunching on a spreadsheet. Within a short space of time, we miraculously got pre-approved for a mortgage, and we moved into our own place a month later.

The most amazing part of this story was that the house we bought was originally on the market at $380,000. Due to the housing downturn, however, it was reduced to $350,000 then $320,000. My hubby told the real estate agent we would put in an offer for $299,000. A couple of days after we made the offer he told me that the real estate agent had called, and our offer had not been accepted. I asked him if he'd made a counteroffer of $310,000 as we had previously discussed. He paused for a moment and said, "Love, I was so busy when she rang me, and I was with a client. When she asked me what our offer was, I just said $299,000 again!"

Oh goodness, I thought to myself. I went to bed that night thinking we might have shot ourselves in the foot. But no, we hadn't—because of our God! The next day, the real estate agent rang and said the offer of $299,000 had been accepted! If we had not taken those steps as best we knew how earlier in the process, I don't believe God would have provided such a miracle.

A similar thing happened when I first took the leap into my own business in my late thirties. I was filled with a mixture of emotions. I knew God was calling me to open my own coaching and consulting practice, and the name He gave me was Propel Consultancy. I love to propel people into action in their business and career pathways. When I first began, all I had was a small amount of savings. But I wasn't going to let that stop me. I soon got my first contract, writing some business education material.

One area I was passionate about was helping students with study skills. I had just finished a fifteen-year teaching career and had wide experience and credibility in the education sector. I decided to devise a series of study skills workshops, wrote up some promotional materials, and sent out some emails. Things started slowly, and I was having nightmares of eating two-minute noodles for the next few months until more cashflow came in. As I was talking with the Father about this, He showed me a picture in my mind's eye of a map. When I asked the Lord what it was about, He said, "Go on a road trip—take your promotional material and go out to the schools in the rural and regional areas that surround the city where you live." That's exactly what I did, and ninety percent of the schools I visited booked me in to present the study skills workshop to their students. Woohoo, I was underway! These workshops led to other gigs and opportunities, and also started to fuel an increasing desire to provide services, programmes, and projects to remote, rural and regional areas, not just metropolitan areas.

Cultivating An Action-Oriented Approach

Action builds momentum, and momentum creates opportunities and opens doors. Here are some practical applications to help you build a more action-orientated approach in your business. You can apply these to your personal and ministry life too.

Planning

Benjamin Franklin famously said, "If you fail to plan, you are planning to fail," and I can attest to the truth of this. Start by creating a ninety-day plan. Ninety days is twelve weeks. Set targets for sales, marketing, clients, strategy, vision, and financial growth. Have no more than four to six targets, but make sure they are very specific.

Processes

As with everything you do in business, work towards creating a process for each of your targets. This will mean that what you do is systemised and automated instead of being reactive and ad hoc. This can take time—but the result is well worth the effort. For example, what process do you follow after you have attended a networking event? I have found that the key with processes is to use a range of digital tools to help you achieve your goals—I have lots of favourites! My top three apps are: Pocket (for collecting articles and information), Trello (where I keep my ideas, planning and client notes), and Easy Voice Recorder (for recording audio on the run). When I am in a hurry, I can speak my notes or blog ideas into the recorder for when I am ready to use it.

Priorities

There are only so many hours in a day, and our business should not consume us. If you own a service-based business, think about how you can productise your services, so that the service becomes a product. The idea is to get you out of the picture and turn your service into a form of passive income. Types of income streams are: active (one to one); leveraged (one to many); a hybrid of active and leverage (e.g., online course but with a Mastermind or Facebook group); passive (e.g., downloadable templates and check sheets); and, recurring (e.g., monthly fees from a membership site or retainer fee for monthly client). As a new business, you will find a lot of your income will initially come from active services—you simply must get runs on the board and get your brand visible and recognised. Make sure people know and understand what it is you do and what you can offer. As your business grows, you can then move to leverage (one to many instead of one to one). The wider goal is to move towards productising so that you have passive and recurring income.

Projects

Plan your business development and growth in terms of projects. Doing this is a good way to keep your ideas flowing but captured, as you can't be working on all your projects at once. As an entrepreneur, you always have ideas flowing, which can be both an advantage and a disadvantage! I have found that putting those ideas into a project format means that even if I don't get around to implementing them straight away, I have a means of retaining those thoughts and plans. Ideally, have no more than two or three projects per quarter, although this will of course depend on the extent of the projects. The next step is to manage the projects. To do this you need to identify what is required for each project, what tools are needed, and who you need to seek help from.

Practise

Over-analysis and anxiety lead to paralysis and procrastination. That's when you become the deer in the headlights! Open the door just a little, even if the key seems stiff in your hand. You have to make a *start*. You will stumble, trip and fall over, but you will rise again! For example, video content marketing is a key marketing method and will continue to be so for some time. If you hate doing videos, start

SHE IS ACTION-ORIENTED

by making a ten-second clip about how you love your cat or dog or children, and send it to a friend. Then build your video confidence muscles from there. Simply take that one step. For example, buy a desk tripod to put your phone on when filming, or purchase a nice scarf or new lipstick to wear while you film. Practise, practise, and practise some more!

~

As a Type-A personality, I have been action-oriented for most of my life, to the point of overdoing it. If I don't keep some healthy boundaries on my 'doing' I can end up being stuck thinking I have to constantly be achieving something. I call this the Martha complex. Here is how Jesus addresses it in Luke 10: 41-42: "Martha, Martha," the Lord answered, "you are worried and upset about many things, but few things are needed—or indeed only one. Mary has chosen what is better, and it will not be taken away from her." In our God we must learn to both *do*—being action-oriented—and *be*—recharging our batteries by soaking in our Lord's presence.

On the other hand, I have met many people who are so focussed on being minimal that no doing, no action, ever happens. To people who might say things like, "I am waiting on God to give me a new job," I ask the question, "Have you updated your CV and written down a list of places you would love to get a job at, and then added some prayer on top of those actions?" They often look at me incredulously and say, "No, I wait on the Lord." Their responses indicate that they think I am being quite unspiritual. However, our inaction brings death to those things that may have been. We have to sow a seed—for instance, update your CV—and then it is God who will water that seed and cause there to be the increase (1 Corinthians 3:6-11)

As with all areas of life, when it comes to action, it is about balance—we can swing too far on both sides of the pendulum. Too much *doing* leads to burnout, too much *being* leads to death of dreams, aspirations and hopes. We need wisdom on what actions to take in each area of our personal, business and ministry life. If we are out of balance, we need to challenge ourselves. For example, do we take lots of action when it comes to business matters, but neglect to be action-orientated when it comes to our health and wellbeing or our money management?

You, Daughter of God reading this book, are called to shift the course of history. This is what stands out for me the most when I read about the life of Deborah—and in fact in many other stories of women in the Bible, such as Esther and Ruth. These women were all history makers. They knew and walked in the call of God on their lives. They actioned the assignments God had put in their hands with bravery, prayer, and boldness.

Maybe you think, "But God, who am I to do such things? I am simply an ordinary woman." You know what? Yes, we are ordinary women, but we are serving, loving and worshipping an extraordinary God. You and God make a majority. 1 Corinthians 1:27 explains that God chooses the foolish things of the world to shame the wise; He chooses the weak things of the world to shame the strong.

Jabin's army was made up of nine-hundred iron chariots, which, in the natural, was a huge force against the ten-thousand men on foot. Yet Barak's army moved in the supernatural, not the natural. They took action only after Deborah prompted them with a prophetic word to do so. And look what happened as a result: history was changed, changed because Deborah chose to stand up and put into action that which God had whispered into her heart.

SHE IS ACTION-ORIENTED

The truth is, right now we only see in part, but one day we will see in full (1 Corinthians 13:12). Actioning what God has spoken to us can be scary at times. We ask, "God, what if I have got it wrong, what I stuff up?" But ask yourself this: what if you've got it right and history will be shifted? This is where you need to step out as Deborah did with boldness and wisdom. You might make mistakes, you might get off track, but God, whose love for you is everlasting, will draw you back. The Holy Spirit will direct you, help you and comfort you. God and you—what an adventure; what a partnership! Mighty modern-day Deborah, it is time for action!

Reflection Questions

1. Look over the section on cultivating an action-orientated approach in your business. For each 'P' word (Planning, Processes, Priorities, Projects, Practise), what will you do to strengthen your business?

2. Now pick one area (e.g. process) and consider what you are going to start with. Give it a try, then reflect and pause. Did it work? Has it helped? What do you need to tweak and change?

3. Connect with a friend and share what is helping you become more action-orientated in your business and the impact that is having. Pray for each other in the areas of action that you are finding most challenging.

4. If you are not in business, apply these P's to your personal or ministry life—and reflect on how you are going to strengthen each one.

A Clarion Call to Modern-Day Deborahs

In Judges 5, the statement "Wake up! Arise!" is uttered four times by Deborah and Barak in their song. God was stirring the hearts of both Deborah and Barak, urging them to sit up straight and pay close attention to what God was about to do. God was communicating that He was about to bring them new revelation and strengthen their calling in Him.

> *"Wake up, wake up, Deborah! Wake up, wake up, break out in song! Arise, Barak! Take captive your captives, son of Abinoam."*
> — *Judges 5:12*

Mighty Deborahs, in this hour we need to be women of vision. There are visions—assignments, projects and tasks—that the Lord wants to show us. I feel that urgency in my spirit like never before. As we look across the nations and see an increase in wars, flooding, famine, strife and destruction, we know that the Day of the Lord is at hand. We can't just sit around waiting. We must go up into our 'watchtowers' to see and hear what the Lord is saying to us for people, places, and nations. We must be strategic and purposeful in looking for opportunities to write, speak, tell and encourage those God has put around us to go and do that which God has put in their hearts.

I will climb up to my watchtower and stand at my guardpost. There I will wait to see what the LORD says and how he will answer my complaint. Then the LORD said to me, "Write my answer plainly on tablets, so that a runner can carry the correct message to others. This vision is for a future time. It describes the end, and it will be fulfilled. If it seems slow in coming, wait patiently, for it will surely take place. It will not be delayed.
— *Habakkuk 2:1-3,* NLT

So often as we journey in our faith we can slip into a place of ease and get lethargic about the call of God on our life. We can start to take things for granted and find ourselves not fully relying on God as we truly want to. Seasons can go by without much devotion to God in worship—prayer and praise—or time in the Word. It's not that we have lost our fire for God or that we are not doing the work of God as we go about our days. It is merely because we are human!

Our humanness means we often fall back into undisciplined ways of doing life, and our calling, our ministry, our faith-filled business becomes 'just another' thing on our to-do list. In these times we do need a wake-up call from God. In a spiritual sense, if we allow the things of the world to block our ears, we become a little deaf to the things of God. Sometimes, we know this is happening, but we carry on all the same.

This can be likened to when we have a small amount of wax in our ears. A small amount may seem not to be a problem, but if we allow the wax to build up, eventually we experience a lot of pain and may need to go to a doctor to get it fully cleaned out. I have had problems with my ears over the years, and my goodness how much clearer it is to hear after a clean-out! Likewise, there are seasons and times in our life when we need God to get on His loudspeaker and call out to us, "Wake up, wake up":

> *"Wake up, wake up, Deborah! Wake up, wake up, break out in song!"*

The day Deborah heard those words in Judges 5:12 was a loudspeaker day!

In writing this book, I felt that God wanted to call to us afresh and strengthen us as modern-day Deborahs. My heart was to urge Christian women entrepreneurs to awaken and arise to all that He has purposed and called us to.

This is a letter I penned from the Father's heart to you, dear reader, dear modern-day Deborah. I declare these words over your life as a clarion call. The word clarion comes from the Latin word *clarus*, meaning, 'loud and clear'. I want today to be a loudspeaker day to you. As you read these words, hear the Father breathing upon the hopes and dreams in your heart once again: *Go!*

> *Dear Daughters,*
>
> *I am roaring from Zion! Come forth, my daughters who are sitting in the shadows. Leave behind your brokenness and discouragement. It is time, time to step—not just a little, but fully—into the calling I have given you. It is time to pioneer. History is at stake. You are my daughters, co-heirs with me, and I am calling you to participate with me in shifting the course of history. Learn to roar! No longer be content to play in the puddles. I call you to stand up, to straighten your battle armour and not let your pain push you down any longer. Open that cage, get out of it, and get flying!*
>
> *I have horizons for you, my daughters, to see. I have places to take you. I have miracles to pour through you. You are not to be*

found sitting in the back row of life. You are not to settle for a life less ordinary. Come and fly with me, your God. As you do the possible, I will do the impossible—over, and over, and over again.

Daughter—timidness, brokenness, hurt, discouragement, and despair have to stop. A line has to be drawn in the sand. I have provided the way through the cross of Calvary. I have shed my blood. I have come to bring life and to bring life abundantly. I am the victor. So daughters, walk in victory. I know, and I understand—I too wept—but the days of weeping are over. It is time to awake and arise.

Mighty Deborahs, arise. It is time for my daughters to go forth boldly. It is time to flip the narrative. The hour of 'softly, softly' is over. I am roaring over you from Zion, "Wake up, wake up, Arise!"

Love,

The Lion of the Tribe of Judah

5+U PILLARS OF BUSINESS MODEL ©

The 5+U Pillars of Business Model © is a series of questions to help you identify the range of matters that you need to consider when starting out in business. If you have already begun your business, you can also use this set of questions to reflect on matters in your business that you have not addressed and/or that you need to sharpen and make changes to.

Pillar 1: Strategic Matters

1. What is your story/background/experiences?

2. What are your skills?

3. What are your passions and interests?

4. What does an ideal 'work/business' day look like for you?

5. What are the business ideas you have?

6. How will you generate income from your business ideas?

7. What income streams will you have?

8. What products can you create from your services?

9. What services can you create from your products?

10. What are the strengths, weaknesses, opportunities and threats of your business ideas?

11. What problem/s will your business solve?

12. What are your business goals—short-term, medium-term, long term?

13. Do you intend to build your business as a saleable asset—and if so, how do you intend to do this over what timeframe?

5+U PILLARS OF BUSINESS MODEL ©

Pillar 2: Legal Compliance Matters

Disclaimer: Please ensure you refer to the legal compliance matters relevant to your own country.

1. Have you registered for a Business Tax Number?

2. Have you registered your Business Name?

3. Have you registered your Domain Name (a URL) for your website and email address?

4. What insurance will you need, for example, Public Liability, Public Indemnity, Vehicle, Inventory

5. What licenses and/or legal permissions do you need, for example, a Food Handling License?

6. What associations/memberships do you need to belong to and/or you would benefit from belonging to?

7. What certificates/training do you need for the products/services your business will provide?

8. What employment contracts, service agreements and/or other legal documentation (for example, a trademark for your logo, a lease for office premises) do you need?

9. What will be the legal structure for your business?

Pillar 3: Marketing Matters

1. Have you conducted market research, that is, is there a demand for your product/service?

2. Who will be your customers/clients?

3. Who will be your ideal customer/client?

4. How much are your customers/clients willing to pay?

5. Who is your competition?

6. Will you have a pilot phase for the business, to test the market?

5+U PILLARS OF BUSINESS MODEL ©

7. What will be your business name, logo, tagline and branding colours?

8. What social media platforms are you going to use?

9. What range of marketing collateral will you have, for example, flyers, brochures, banners, business cards, car magnets, fridge magnets, promotional products (e.g., keyring, USB, hat, pen)?

10. Will you create a Business Capability Statement and/or portfolio to showcase your business?

11. What will be your four or five marketing actions each week?

12. What type of website (for example, e-commerce so that you can sell products) do you want?

Pillar 4: Operational Matters, including Human Resources and IT

1. Where will you run your business from?

2. What equipment and/or stock do you need for your business?

3. What are the risks associated with running your business?

4. What staff will you need for the business?

5. What will be your operating procedures?

6. What will be your recruitment and induction processes?

7. Have you created an email account for the business?

8. What computer/IT equipment do you need?

9. How will you take electronic payments?

10. What apps will you use in your business to increase efficiency?

11. What voice message and email signature will you have?

5+U PILLARS OF BUSINESS MODEL ©

Pillar 5: Financial Matters

1. Have you opened a separate bank account/s for your business?

2. What will be your recordkeeping processes?

3. What accounting software will you use?

4. Have you found a bookkeeper/accountant to help guide your business financial matters?

5. What financial documents do you need, for example, receipts, quotes, invoices etc?

6. What will be your Terms and Conditions of payment, charging of deposits, terms of credit?

7. Are you aware of your tax obligations?

8. What will be your financial processes policies, for example, Debt Collection Policy?

9. What are your projected expenses and sales for the business?

10. What wage/salary will you pay yourself from the business?

Pillar U (You): You, the Business Owner

1. Who will you have as the 'cheer squad' for your business?

2. What coaching/mentoring will you participate in?

3. What networking opportunities align with your business?

4. What computer skills do you have and what computer skills do you need to learn?

5. What professional development/skills building do you need to do?

6. What will self-care as a business owner look like for you?

5+U PILLARS OF BUSINESS MODEL ©

7. How many weeks in a year do you intend to run your business?

8. What breaks do you plan to take and how will you ensure the business still runs well during those break times?

9. What personal areas in your life do you need to get some professional support on navigating as they may impact you as a business owner, for example, anxiety in networking situations?

Maree Cutler-Naroba
Copyright 2023 ©

About the Author

MAREE IS A MULTI-PASSIONATE woman who loves to serve people, through the gifts and talents God has placed in her hands, as a prophetic pioneer for His Kingdom. Maree outworks the call of God on her life through a plethora of business and ministry ventures.

Through her business, *MCN Consulting*, Maree offers a variety of business strategic planning and entrepreneur education services to assist businesses to position themselves for impact and legacy. One of the specialities of MCN Consulting is supporting women living in remote, rural or regional areas. Additionally, as a multidisciplinary, trauma-informed practitioner, Maree focuses on working with clients, communities and organisations for whom the application of a trauma-informed lens is central to their growth and development.

www.mcn-consulting.com

MCN Consulting has four sister businesses, *Mind that Gap Studio* (content and course creation for service professionals), *Swirl* (online business coaching and design services for midlife professional women), *MCN Dream Nurturer* (supporting women to turn their adversity into service) and *Boomers Biz Gym* (entrepreneur education and coaching for new business owners 50+).

https://mcn-consulting.com.au/mind-that-gap-studio/

www.justswirl.com.au

www.mareecutlernaroba.com

https://www.facebook.com/boomersinbizforacause

Maree founded *The Deborah Conference* as a tool to inspire Christian Women Entrepreneurs to live a business life of passionate pursuit and purpose wrapped in His presence. This conference sits within the *Deborah Business Education Hub* which focuses on Christ-centred business education. The DBEH provides support, inspiration, impartation and prayer to champion the faith-filled business journey of Christian Women Entrepreneurs, and includes *Deborah Women in Business Collective* chapters which assist in developing micro business ventures of rural women in developing nations.

www.thedeborahconference.com

www.deborohbizedhub.com

https://deborahbizedhub.com/dwib-collective/

The Women Echo Him Collective (WEHC), founded by Maree, is a global community of women who put the 'trumpet' to their lips, praying and declaring God's heartbeat over towns, cities and nations.

www.wehcollective.com

ABOUT THE AUTHOR

The Barnabas Legacy Children's Dream Foundation (BLCDF) is a legally registered Ugandan Not for Profit Organisation, Jinja, Uganda. Maree is a Director and Board Chair of BLCDF and co-founder of the *Agape Star Christian School,* which sits under the Foundation.

www.barnabaslegacy.org

https://barnabaslegacy.org/agape-star-christian-school/

The *Reily Foundation Inc (South Australia)* is a Foundation whose aim is to strengthen families navigating the child protection system. Maree is currently the Chair of the Foundation.

www.thereily.foundaiton

www.ingramcontent.com/pod-product-compliance
Lightning Source LLC
Chambersburg PA
CBHW050316010526
44107CB00055B/2260